EVEN DEATH CAN'T STOP ME

Therefore, if anyone is in Christ,
he is a new creation;
old things have passed away;
behold, all things have become new.
—2 Corinthian 5:17 NKJV

Advance Praise for RISE: Even Death Can't Stop Me

"The human spirit is an unparalleled force of nature. Frank Thomas proves that no matter where you come from, the mistakes you've made, or how many times you've failed, when you decide to RISE...even death can't stop you!"

–Bill Bartmann,
CEO of CFS II, 2013 Nobel Peace Prize nominee
and Author of Bouncing Back

"RISE is a powerful testimony of how God can turn your tragedy into triumph when you are willing to surrender to His love, grace and mercy. Frank's story will inspire you to walk in the authority given to those in Christ and fulfill your God-ordained destiny."

–Jesse Bailey,
Lead Pastor of New Wine Family Church,
Woodland Hills, CA

"God is a God of many chances. That's why Frank Thomas is able to tell his powerful story of forgiveness, redemption, and transformation. Through all of the shame, disappointment, and fear, Frank was able to RISE. This is a must read book if you desire to do the same."

–Gary Cooper,
Pastor, Life Coach, and Ministry Leader
of The Alliance

"RISE is a beautiful story about overcoming adversity, discovering the light that exists within each of us, and deciding to become who we were truly created to be. By living authentically and trusting in something greater than ourselves, we not only change internally, but we have the power to change the world. A MUST READ!"

–Cali Gilbert,
#1 International Bestselling Author & Creator
of the IT'S SIMPLY Book Series

RISE

EVEN DEATH CAN'T STOP ME

FRANK THOMAS

MASCOT BOOKS

Mascot Books
560 Herndon Parkway #120
Herndon, VA 20170
info@mascotbooks.com

For information about special discounts for bulk purchases, please contact
Mascot Books at 1-703-437-3584.

Frank Thomas is available to speak at your live event. For more information
or to book an event, contact the author's agent at 1-818-854-4491 or visit
his website at www.coachft.com.

Cover design by Aaron Coleman
Cover photo by Dan McCollister

PRBVG0115A

Library of Congress Control Number: 2014919273

ISBN-13: 9781620865897

Printed in the United States

www.mascotbooks.com

"Honor your father and your mother, that your days may be long upon the land which the Lord your God is giving you."
—Exodus 20:12 NKJV

This book is dedicated to my mother.
No matter what we've gone through,
I will always love and honor you.
I can't imagine the pain you've endured.
You fought like a champion.
You taught me how to battle.
Rest now.
I'll finish it from here, Mom.
This is my tribute to you.

CONTENTS

AUTHOR'S NOTE

This is a work of nonfiction. I have rendered the events faithfully and truthfully just as I have recalled them. Some names and descriptions of individuals have been changed in order to respect their privacy. To anyone whose name I did not recall or omitted, I offer sincere apologies. While circumstances and conversations depicted herein come from my keen recollection of them, they are not meant to represent precise time lines of events or exact word-for-word reenactments of my life. They are told in a way that evokes the real feeling and meaning of what was said and my view of what happened to me, in keeping with the true essence of the mood and spirit of those moments that shaped my life.

INTRODUCTION

BIGGER THAN ME

"Let the redeemed of the Lord tell their story, those He redeemed from the hand of the foe." Psalm 107:2 NIV

Have you ever done something so awful that you kept it hidden from others because you believed that if they knew they'd judge you harshly? Have you ever had something so horrible happen to you that you vowed to never share it with anyone? Almost everyone has made an embarrassing mistake, done something wrong, or has had something so ugly happen to them that they swore to conceal it out of shame. Shame derives its power from the silence and darkness of secrecy.

For much of my life, I kept secrets because of my shame. I had shame because I was born to a 16-year-old unwed mother who had two kids by the time she was 18. I had shame because I grew up in poverty. I had shame because my father was a junkie who spent my childhood in prison. I had shame because my life was overrun by violence, addiction, depression, low self-esteem, hopelessness and the feelings of always struggling. Yet I always hid my shame and made others believe I was happy. I became a Jedi Master at manipulating people's perception of me because of my insecurity and fear. But deep within, I felt ugly, insecure, and worthless.

I feared that if people really knew me—if they knew how I had been raised, the mistakes I'd made, or the horrible things I'd done—they would reject me. So I hid because I didn't want to be alone.

The problem is, not only did I hide my shame in darkness, but I hid my light too. You must choose which one you will serve. To hide my shame meant that I was its prisoner. Whenever I found the courage to do something bold that would illuminate and fulfill my God-given purpose, the thought of being exposed, humiliated, and rejected would envelop my mind and cause me to freeze in fear. My shame would tell me to sit down and shut my mouth before everything about me was revealed in the light.

But I finally realized something: the fear of being rejected because of your failures or mistakes only keeps you playing small in life. It's in this fact that I finally understood the only way I was going to ever break free from my shame and fear was to go public with the very things I was striving to keep a secret. If I didn't, I would continue to be held hostage in the prison of my mind. No matter how much success I'd achieved, I, ultimately, left success on the table because I held back out of fear. For years I lived smaller than the purpose God created me for and I was frustrated.

When I was an adolescent, I had dreams that I would do something with my life as significant as Dr. Martin Luther King Jr. had done with his. I knew I had that kind of power. Yet I felt stifled. I didn't know how to access the power within me but I knew it was there; it was undeniable. But shame kept me in check. When I tried to overcome it, unconsciously, I let it sabotage me instead. I would latch on to anyone who showed me any kind of love or attention, even if it was damaging. If I didn't get the validation I craved, my emotions would spiral out of control with insecurity and I would act out in destructive ways: alcohol abuse, sex, fighting, and the love and pursuit of money.

By the time I was 11 years old, money had become my drug of choice. I believed that money was the answer to everything. When I had money I felt powerful. When I didn't I felt worthless, hopeless, and needy. So when my mother became a drug dealer and opened the door to fast money in amounts I could've never imagined, I walked right through. I had yet to learn the street proverb that all money isn't good money.

Three weeks into my drug-dealing experience I was arrested and charged with a felony. I ultimately pled guilty and was sentenced to two years probation. The events of my arrest and conviction were a wakeup call and compelled me to move away from my family in the Midwest to start a new life in Southern California. But just as things were beginning to look up, my whole world came crashing down. On a visit back to my hometown, I was caught in a drug raid and arrested for possession of drugs that belonged to my mother. Put to the test, she turned her back and abandoned me. Facing up to 60 years in prison for her actions, I was left to fight for my life. With nowhere else to turn, my only refuge was in a God that I didn't really know. It was in a jail cell where I sat awaiting trial that I received Jesus as my personal Lord and Savior, transforming my life. Almost instantaneously, I went from being a scared little boy to a man who knew God created him with a purpose and a destiny that was far beyond my circumstances.

After a lengthy and hard fought court battle I was sent to prison. Upon my release, I returned to Southern California, once again, to start anew. At 20 years old, and carrying around a felony conviction, all I had was my faith, ambition, and dreams of a better life. But, things would prove difficult, as my criminal record made it nearly impossible to find employment.

Doors were shut in my face. I was rejected for the mistake I made even though I was trying to do all the right things. I couldn't bear the thought of being judged for the rest of my life for a mistake I'd made when I was a desperate, irresponsible teenager. I didn't want people to stereotype me as just another young black male who had been to prison. So I went into hiding; I lied about my past. When the time came to fill out the next job application and I was confronted with the frightening question, "Have you ever been convicted of a felony?" I lied, and I got the job.

I worked hard for that company and received several promotions along the way. But one day I had a revelation that it was time for me go higher. That meant I needed a formal education—a college degree. Despite being a convicted felon, I had never viewed myself as a criminal. I'd made a horrible mistake but in my heart I knew I was a good and hard-working person. I still believed that I could do something great with my life.

I ended up at the University of Southern California on a partial academic scholarship. I graduated with a degree in accounting and was the student commencement speaker at my graduation. Deloitte & Touche, the second largest professional services firm in the world, hired me. I became a licensed Certified Public Accountant (CPA) and eventually a corporate executive for a Fortune 500 company. But, I was still hiding my felony conviction from everyone except my employers because of shame.

Then in 2010, I became the executive director of a nonprofit social services organization that helped educate and influence at-risk youth to make good choices that positively impact their future. It was a calling and labor of love. However, due to the economic recession and state budget cuts, the organization was faced with a major funding shortfall. I had intended to use my knowledge and business experience to turn the organization's financial condition around. But it didn't take me long before I realized that it was going to take a major overhaul of the entire organization—and a miracle—in order to save it.

During this time, I would look into the eyes of the underprivileged youth we served and they looked familiar. They looked just like me when I was their age. They were fighting the shame of poverty, low self-esteem, and lack of support from family. Many of them were acting out: getting into trouble with the law, abusing drugs and alcohol, being sexually promiscuous and joining gangs. These kids needed the love, discipline, hope and vision that the organization was trying to provide. But without the financial resources, the days of our ability to champion their cause were numbered.

Faced with the growing challenge of raising enough money to keep the organization in operation, I received another revelation: "Tell your story." That led me to believe that the only possible way to save the organization—and the kids who needed it—was based on my willingness to humble myself and tell the story I had been trying to conceal my entire life. I was the poster boy for the organization's mission, and I believed it was the only way to reach people who had the means and heart to help save our kids.

In November 2010, I got the courage to tell my story of poverty, despair, addiction, imprisonment and perseverance as a speaker at a business event. Wonder of wonders, at the end of that function, there was a line of people waiting to speak with me. Several people were crying and they shared how deeply my story had touched them. Others told me how they had overcome challenges of their own and that my story reminded them of the strength they had needed. Others were facing life's difficulties at that moment and said they had been inspired by my courage. That was the day I became conscious of my story's power and I knew I could no longer be selfish by hiding it. That was the day I realized that my story was bigger than me.

In fact, it wasn't my story at all. It was God's story, and He was planning to use it for His glory—to bring freedom to those who have been incarcerated in the prison of their minds because of shame.

When the dust settled, the nonprofit organization still closed its doors. I've had the opportunity to reflect on that and now I see clearly. God never sent me to save that organization. He sent that organization to save me. Without it, I believe that my story would've died with me and I would've died a prisoner to my shame. In the Bible, Romans 8:28 KJV says, "And we know that all things work together for good to them that love God, to them who are the called according to his purpose." I get it now. God had taken my mess and made a message.

How did I find the courage to tell my story? I finally understood that my true identity was in Christ Jesus and nothing else. I had been overcompensating, trying to create an identity and achieve my worth through my performance: earning degrees, big job titles, and money. That worked great when I was achieving and performing at a high level. But failure is an inevitable part of life. When I failed I would wither and my self-esteem would evaporate. It took me years and many mistakes to understand an important key to living the life God created us for: our worth is not determined by anything except the reality that Jesus Christ died for our sins. Our worth is inherent in His sacrifice. It's not based on our performance, our wealth, our looks, race, gender, or anything else. He decided it the day He willingly went to the cross for you and me.

If you're a believer that Jesus Christ is the Son of God and came to earth in human form to die for the sins of the world, own the power and authority you've been given through His blood. Own your imperfections and tell your story. Revelations 12:11 KJV says, "And they overcame him by the blood of the lamb, and by the word of their testimony..." Jesus already did His part. The rest is up to us. There are people who need to hear our testimonies. They need to know they can move beyond, grow from and be redeemed from their worst mistakes or the horrible things that have happened to them. They need to know that those things don't have to become their identity. People need to hear less about our self-proclaimed successes and more about how we were saved by God's grace through Christ Jesus. People don't want to be around perfect people. People want to be around people who are imperfect just like they are but who know they have been saved by grace.

The world is looking for leadership and no one's coming. You're it, in Christ Jesus. Now, RISE!

PART ONE

The Fall

CHAPTER 1

CRACK

In the late 1980s and early '90s, there was a war going on in the streets of every major city across the United States. Crack cocaine—a potent and cheap narcotic—had been introduced to the American drug culture and ripped its way across the country, devastating families and entire communities, primarily those of color.

Crack—coupled with poverty, violence and a general sense of hopelessness—decimated the African-American community during this period, and my family was right in the middle of it all. My father, mother, brother and I have all been convicted of drug felonies and been on the wrong side of a prison cell. I lived through crack's destructive effect on the black community and watched as it mercilessly destroyed my dreams and tore my family apart.

Throughout my youth, there were countless junctures where my life could have dramatically changed or even ended. But none was more gripping than a spring day in April 1991 in Des Moines, Iowa. I was 19 years old, and I had no idea that my life was about to be altered forever.

A week earlier, I'd received a call from my mother at my home in San Diego. I had moved there from Des Moines less than two months earlier after receiving probation for pleading guilty to a felony for selling crack cocaine on a local street corner in October of 1990. Just about everyone in my family was either an alcoholic, drug abuser, drug dealer, ex-con or all of the above. Drugs, alcohol, violence, and prison were my family's norm. I knew I had to get away while I still had a life to save.

Now it appeared I would have to go back. During the phone call, my mother informed me that I had been summoned to appear at a deposition in Kansas City, Missouri, to give testimony in an ongoing lawsuit, the result of a multi-car, high-speed collision my brother, Montez, and I were in when I was 16. I was the driver and my younger brother was my passenger. Neither of us was wearing a seatbelt and were both nearly ejected from the car into oncoming traffic. By the grace of God, we walked away with our lives.

Legal proceedings had been dragging on for nearly four years and finally appeared to be coming to a close. Due to property damage, injuries, and the fact that I was not at fault, we believed that the court would award us a small fortune. So I prepared myself to make the journey from San Diego back to the Midwest. I would drive to Des Moines to pick up my mother and then drive to Kansas City to give my sworn testimony. Once the deposition was complete, I would drop my mother back in Des Moines, and make my way back to San Diego.

The Man

On the day of my trip, I woke up a few hours before dawn and began the 1,700-mile drive across the country. I had recently purchased a soft top 1987 turquoise blue Suzuki Samurai and outfitted it with two twelve-inch subwoofers, a high-end Rockford Fosgate amplifier and a top-of-the-line Kenwood pullout receiver. You could hear the bass from three blocks away. I wanted to drive into Des Moines with my bangin' car, loud sound system and California license plates. Everyone was going to think I was "the man"; I couldn't wait to see the looks on their faces.

I completed the drive in twenty-seven hours. Several times I nodded off at the wheel, only to be awakened by the vibration and rumbling of the tires rolling over the sleeper lines. Still, I wouldn't stop. That was something I'd learned from my mother. She was strong-willed, tough and stubborn. When she focused her mind on something, nothing would stand in her way. That trait must have been genetic, because I inherited it.

I pulled into the driveway of my grandmother's house on 18th Street, where my mother lived with my father, my uncle Michael, my aunt Kim and a couple of my cousins. I did so with mixed emotions. A year earlier, my mother and father had gotten back together after about ten years. During that time, my father did several stints in prison, mostly a result of his addiction to drugs. During that same period, my mother's life had slowly disintegrated and she had come full circle, back to the city and the man she and her two young boys fled a decade earlier.

This time, though, it was drugs and fast cash that brought them together. By April 1991, my mother had been dealing drugs for well over a year and was addicted to the money. The escape from years of poverty had restored her spark and swagger, but the combination of drugs, alcohol, money and bad choices was to prove explosive.

Flossin'

I walked through the side door of the house that led into the kitchen. My grandmother was sitting at the table drinking a beer and playing solitaire, just like she did every day. My cousin Keith was sitting on a bar stool at the kitchen counter talking to her. As I walked through the door, they both glanced at me with eyes wide.

"Oh snap! Your girl dumped you already?" Keith asked. Always one to punch below the belt. I laughed it off and gave my grandmother a hug and kiss. The remainder of my family began to file into the kitchen upon hearing the commotion and we exchanged hugs. Even though I had moved away from all of them a couple months earlier, they were still my family and I loved them. What made the trip bearable was knowing I didn't have to stay. They're a jovial and witty clan, who knew how to make me laugh, but I didn't want to get pulled back into their way of life.

After hanging out for a while, I decided to jump into my car and ride around the city "flossin'"—showing off. Everywhere I drove around Des Moines, people could hear me coming from several blocks away. As I drove by I would nod my head as if to say, "What up?" to everyone I passed.

While out cruising, I ran into my cousin Jamal. Jamal was one of the city's biggest drug dealers and a known leader of the Crips gang in Des Moines. He was hanging out at a park off of Forest Avenue near my old stomping grounds, TNT Lounge, a local bar and one of the major hotspots for drug activity. TNT Lounge was also the scene of my arrest six months prior that led to a felony conviction. As I pulled into the park smiling, expecting to be greeted with a hug, Jamal gave me a stern warning instead.

"Man, you need to quit riding around in that thing with those California plates," he said. "The Po-Po are going to end up jackin' you up."

He was right. I'd known more than a few people who'd had drugs planted in their vehicles by the police and been wrongly arrested. I didn't trust the cops. Being on probation meant I couldn't put myself in a situation where I could even look questionable. I headed back to my grandmother's house and parked my car.

Later that evening, I got a surprise visit from my older cousin, Aaron, who had heard I was in town. He wanted to see if I was interested in hanging out that night. Since I was only going to be in town for a few days, I decided to take him up on the offer.

"Hey Mom! I'm leaving!" I shouted so that she could hear me in the upstairs bedroom. The door to the bedroom opened and I could hear her making her way downstairs.

"Hold on," she said as she descended. "Let me borrow your car." I paused. It wasn't a question. Part of me really didn't want to let her—not because she wasn't a good driver but because of the possibility of someone else— mainly my Dad—getting the keys and deciding to "rent" it out for drugs to some drug dealer. I had seen that happen several times with my grandmother's car. My father didn't care. His only concern was getting high. But reluctantly, I handed my mother the keys and took off.

Wrongly Accused

The next day when I returned, I was relieved to see my car sitting in the driveway. I went into the kitchen where my grandma was sitting at the table, smoking her long skinny cigarettes, drinking a beer and playing solitaire.

"Hey Grandma."

"Hey baby," she said with a smile.

"Where's my mom?"

I assumed she would tell me my mom was upstairs because I'd seen my car parked in the driveway on my way into the house.

"She ran an errand."

"Was she driving?" I asked.

"Yeah. She took my car."

It struck me as odd that my mother had asked to borrow my car, yet she was driving my grandma's car to run an errand.

"She told me she'd be right back," my grandmother added.

Good. I thought to myself. I'd planned to meet my cousin Aaron down at the gym to play basketball and I needed the keys to my car to get there.

I ran upstairs to change into my gym clothes. Minutes later, I heard my mother enter the house. I went downstairs and into the kitchen where my mother and grandmother were talking.

"Hey mom."

"Hey honey," she replied.

"Can I get my keys from you? I'm about to run down to the gym and play basketball with Aaron."

She dug inside her purse, pulled out my keys and handed them to me. As I got ready to walk out the door she stopped me.

"Before you go, can you help me? I accidentally locked the keys in the car," she said with a sigh.

I put my car keys in the pocket of my gym shorts and went out to see if I could help. With my hands and face pressed against the glass of the driver's side door, I looked inside Grandma's car to see if I could spot the keys. There was no trace of them on the seat, floorboard or in the ignition. The car also had sliding locks on the door panels, so there was no way that I was going to be able to unlock them with a hanger. I began to walk toward the house to tell my mother she was going to have to call a locksmith, when I heard someone yell.

"Freeze!"

Startled, I looked up. A group of white men in dark jackets with big yellow letters that spelled "D-E-A" were running toward me with guns drawn. I panicked. My instincts told me to run. I burst through the side door of the house, ran past my grandmother sitting at the kitchenette and into the living room. I dove onto the floor and buried my face in the carpet. If I was about to be shot, I didn't want to see it.

Seconds later, I could hear the men scrambling through the side door of the house behind me shouting, "Police! Freeze! Freeze!" My grandmother screamed. The police rushed to secure the house and everyone in it. My eyes were clamped shut, but I could feel the guns pointed at me as I lay on the floor, terrified.

Once the police had accounted for everyone in the house, they began to search the property. Everyone was frisked and searched for weapons, drugs and paraphernalia. I lay on the floor for what felt like hours. I didn't know what to think. I just wanted to survive this nightmare.

Then one of the cops kicked my foot. "Stand up!" he ordered. As I got to my feet, he patted me down. He pulled the car keys out of the pocket of my basketball shorts and asked, "Is that your blue jeep in the driveway?"

"Yes."

"Do you mind if we search it?"

"No." I replied. Knowing I had nothing to hide.

I was ordered to lie back on the ground. I did exactly as I was told. Several minutes later I heard one of the cops shout, "Jackpot! Blue Suzuki!"

Immediately, the officer who'd searched my car came back inside.

"Stand up!"

Again, I complied.

"You're under arrest!"

"What?" I said in disbelief. The officer grabbed my arms, cuffed my wrists and read me my Miranda rights. "But, I didn't do anything!" I protested. "I didn't do anything sir! I didn't do anything!" I was on the verge of a breakdown. I could hear the other cops celebrating finding drugs and money in my car.

That's impossible! I thought. Then something horrifying occurred to me. Unless my mother... my mind stopped racing. I knew that she had planted drugs in my car. But there was no time to dwell on that as my father, my cousin Keith, and I were pushed into the back of a paddy wagon and taken to jail. Little did I know at the time, but I was about to be in the fight of my life.

CHAPTER 2

SET UP TO FAIL

The most important factor influencing a child's success or failure in life is the story they inherit from their parents. Children can't determine to whom they're born or how prepared their mother and father are for parenthood. But, we know that children born to happily married, educated, adult parents with secure homes have a higher probability of success than those born to teenaged high school dropouts with no partner. Children of unwed teenage mothers have a higher likelihood of poverty, lack of education, drug addiction and incarceration, and the deck is even more stacked for failure when that young mother has more than one child.

So I had more than one strike against me on July 9, 1971 when, at 12:13am at Broadlawns Polk County Hospital in Des Moines, Iowa, my 16-year-old unwed mother gave birth to me, starting a story of struggle she couldn't possibly have understood. Twenty-one months later, the same series of unwise choices would culminate in the birth of a second little boy—this one born prematurely and with physical deformities that would need multiple surgeries during the first few years of his young life. With no father to help and few role models to guide her, my young mother—herself a product of the foster care system—would be forced to grow up too quickly. Life would punish her and us for her youthful mistakes. From the outset we were set up to fail.

The End of Bliss

Children begin life in ignorant bliss. They're oblivious to good and bad, rich and poor, black and white. Every child's norm is whatever circumstances they are born into. As a young kid, I lived in this blissful state, too—for a while.

But as I got older though, I started to notice differences between my family and others.

Most notably, many of my friends lived in homes where their fathers were present. My dad, on the other hand, was scarcely ever around. One of my earliest memories of him was visiting him at the maximum security Iowa State Penitentiary in Fort Madison, a three-hour drive away from our home in Des Moines.

Before we could see my dad, we'd be searched. Unbeknownst to me at the time, there were people who would use their children to smuggle drugs and other contraband into prisons. I was four years old; I had no idea. I just wanted to see my dad. So I did what I was told.

Once searched, we were led into a large, neatly organized, brightly lit room with several tables and chairs. The guard would direct us where to sit and we would wait with great anticipation for the inmates to be escorted into the visitor's room. When we saw my father, his eyes would light up, and he would grin. He would hurry over to the table to kiss my mother and embrace his boys.

The room was loud, but the love was palpable. Men and women were gazing into each other's eyes. Fathers were talking with and hugging their children. Everything was beautiful during the visit, which usually lasted three or four hours. But once the guard gave a warning call notifying us that visiting hours would be ending soon, the room transformed. Smiles and laughter turned into grieving. I couldn't help but notice tears dropping from my mother's eyes. I didn't see her cry very often so when I did it hurt me deeply. I can only imagine what she was feeling. Not only was she leaving the love of her life behind, but this 20- or 21-year old woman—still a child, really—was forced to go back to being the sole provider and caregiver of two boys—a difficult responsibility for even the most mature of women.

With my father in prison, my mother carried the load without complaint but with little support. She was the only one of her six siblings who had been forced to live in foster care, and she'd always felt like the black sheep of her family. She isolated herself from her siblings, cutting herself off from those who could have been the most help to her.

Still, she was a warrior with a vision of giving her boys a better life. She was young, strong-willed and naïve enough to believe she could make it. She didn't know how to quit; being on her own with two kids gave her a cause worth fighting for. She would not let her kids be taken away from her like her parents allowed her to be taken. Her pride and pain would not let her surrender.

As a result, she learned never to depend on others for anything—to do without before asking others for help, another trait I would also inherit. But giving my brother and me a decent life didn't come easy. We were always lacking something: shoes, clothes, a place of our own and many things that other people take for granted. As I got older, I felt poor in comparison to the other kids. They had toys, bikes, and nice clothes. One of my cousins teased me for wearing corduroy pants in the middle of summer. But the way my mom saw it, at least we had clothes.

Our situation sparked a spirit of survival in me. I wanted to find a way to change our situation and be like the other kids. That would require craftiness on my part. Growing up, Jerry Lewis held an annual Labor Day telethon to raise money for the Muscular Dystrophy Association (MDA). When I was around seven years old, friends and I went door-to-door to every apartment in our complex to collect donations from residents for the MDA. The money never made it past the candy store. That was hardly the last time we came up with a scheme to try and help our living situation.

Home Alone

From the time I was seven, Montez and I were left at home alone during our summer vacations. My mother had to work and I was expected to be responsible for my brother. During those long summer days, she had strict rules: no going outside, no answering the door, and no answering the telephone unless the phone rang our secret code. That secret code consisted of two consecutive rings, and then the caller would have to hang up and call back immediately. If you called our house without knowing that code, you would never speak to us. So when my mother called using the code, we answered. If we didn't, we knew she'd be on her way to find out why, and she'd be angry. We feared our mother's wrath. She was no one to mess with.

My mother knew we were too young to be left at home all day without supervision. But there was no money for summer camp or a babysitter. She figured keeping us locked up all day was the best way to keep us from getting into trouble. However, spending our summer days cooped up in our apartment was rough. We just wanted to play outdoors with the other kids, not be confined like our father in a prison, waiting for yard time!

Well, boys will be boys, won't they? We found ways around our mother's rules. We would take our chances—sneak out or invite our friends over to play.

One day, my friend Jimmy came over to our apartment. He was a white kid who lived in the building next door, and he was about two years older than me. We played together when my mother was home. I knew that I shouldn't have let him in; it was an outright violation of the rules. But Montez and I were bored. Still, I was careful to sneak Jimmy in and to keep the noise down while he visited; our mother always told us she had neighbors watching our every move. I didn't know if that was true, but I wasn't taking any chances.

"Hey," Jimmy said. "I know an apartment in your building where the windows are always unlocked. No one is home during day. They have a bunch of rolled up coins on the shelf in the living room. We should go get them."

I'm not sure why I thought this was a good idea. All my seven-year-old self could think about was all the candy we could buy. So, I agreed. My younger brother did what I did by default. I was the oldest and made the decisions. I turned to Jimmy and said, "Okay. Let's go."

Jimmy led us out of our apartment, down the stairs, and to the front window of the first floor apartment. Slowly and quietly, Jimmy slid the windowpane open and climbed in. Montez was next, and I followed. Jimmy went right to the rolled-up coins; I wasn't far behind. However, as Jimmy was packing coins into his pockets, I saw something in my peripheral vision. A door opened at the end of the dim hallway and a white woman wearing what looked like pajamas saw me and shouted, "Hey!" She began to run toward us.

I panicked, turned around and dashed for the open window. "Hey!" the lady screamed again. I jumped through that open window like an Olympic hurdler and did not look back. My only hope was that Jimmy and my little brother were right behind me. Heart pounding, I ran all the way back to our second floor apartment, slammed the door and locked it, then closed the curtains. Hoping Montez and Jimmy had gotten away too, I sat motionless on the sofa, awaiting their return. Several minutes passed and nobody showed up. My mind raced. I could only assume the worst. After 30 excruciating minutes, there was a knock on the door.

"Frank, open the door," my younger brother sniffled. Whatever was on the other side of that door wasn't good. I opened the door and there stood my brother, in tears, with a police officer holding his arm. My mother is going to kill us! I thought.

"Come with me," the officer commanded as he grabbed my arm. He led us down to the first floor apartment where the woman lived. Shame began to overcome me. I feared looking this woman in the eyes and facing the consequences of our actions. As soon as we entered her doorway she said, "Yep! That's him!"

The officer looked at me, "What's your mother's name and work number?"

"Please," I begged. "Please don't call my mother," tears flowing down my face. I was more afraid to give him my mother's phone number than I was to go to jail.

"I'm sorry," I stuttered as I sobbed. "I promise we won't do it again. I promise." I knew we were dead if my mother found out. Not only did we break her rules, we broke the law. She was not going to put up with that. This was what my mother was trying hard to prevent. She didn't want us to end up like our father.

The officer was unmoved. "Son, what's your mother's name and work number?" he asked again. There was no getting around it. With no other choice, I gave him her name and number. He immediately called my mother and explained what happened. My mother wasted no time. She was home with frightening quickness.

The officer explained the details to her, and my mother apologized to the lady whose apartment we had broken into. She made us apologize as well. The officer then released us to her. My mother took us home. It would be the first time that I did something bad but didn't get whipped for it. I don't know if it was because our mother was so upset that she was afraid she might really hurt us if she whipped us, but she did nothing. That was worse. Knowing how angry and disappointed she was in me hurt more than a beating ever could have. I was disappointed in myself.

Several days later, we were taken downtown to the Polk County Courthouse to answer for what we did. I was terrified because I thought they were going to take us away from our mom. My cousins had told us that if the authorities took us away, we'd go to juvenile hall where they beat you three times a day. Thank goodness my mother worked for the Polk County Attorney's office at the time. She knew a lot of the prosecutors and other people in law enforcement. She had them talk to us and warn us what could happen if they ever saw us for something like that again. We promised they wouldn't. It was just a scare tactic, but an effective one. We were let go with a harsh warning. We'd been lucky.

Dad Comes Home

As I was growing up, several events gave glimpses into my future, though I was too young to understand them. The rolled coins caper was one. Another was my father being paroled from prison and coming home in the summer of 1980. Montez and I were too young to understand his troubles. Innately, we just knew we needed him. My mother would get up each morning for work and Montez and I got to spend some time with our dad. We loved this.

One day, Montez and I were in the bedroom we shared playing Monopoly. My father happened to come in and see us playing. He immediately dropped to the floor where we sat, picked up the dice and began to shake them. The dice made a clicking noise so melodic it was mesmerizing. He released the dice and shouted, "Seven!"—as the dice rolled a four, two and two. Again, he picked up the dice, shook them in his hand and rolled them. "Little Joe!" he shouted. I watched him, dazzled.

Suddenly, he grabbed the Monopoly money and divided it equally among the three of us. This would become our first official lesson in craps. Not only did we learn the rules of the game, my Dad taught us the mannerisms as well. As we rolled the dice, we'd snap our fingers on release and shout, "Seven!" The fake money was changing hands quickly. We were thrilled with the new game. Never mind that it was gambling; it was one of the only things my father ever taught me. His only other lesson would come more than a decade later, and not heeding it would cost me dearly.

But now, for the first time in my life, I felt like we had a family. Life was good, at least for a while. We had our own apartment with furniture and food in the refrigerator. However, after too short a time, tumultuous events would force my mother to make a decision that would change our lives forever.

Late one evening my mother came home in a panic. I heard the front door open and footsteps walk down the hallway to the bedroom my brother and I shared. I lifted my head as the door opened. From the shape of the silhouette, I could tell that it was my mother looking in on us. Feeling a sense of comfort, I lay down and went back to sleep.

Minutes later, I was startled awake by the sound of crying. I jumped out of bed and ran into the living room. There my mother sat on the sofa sobbing. Not knowing what was going on, I quickly ran to the sofa and hugged her.

"Mommy, what's wrong?" I bawled. She tried to speak, but nothing came out. Then I noticed a white piece of paper in her hands. I'd seen the paper sitting on the coffee table in the days leading up to that night. Written on it was a poem that referred to some kind of drug, but I couldn't understand more than that.

"This is what has your dad," my mom said simply, like a judge passing a sentence. I sat there perplexed, gazing at the paper. The pain in my mother's voice crushed me.

The next morning, I noticed that all of the windows in my mother's car had been shattered. My dad didn't come home that night, or any night after that. I wouldn't see him again for ten years. In the weeks that followed, it became clear that the poem referred to heroin, the drug my father was addicted to.

I found out that on that evening, my mom had seen my dad at a local nightclub. He was with another woman. She confronted him, and an altercation ensued. My mom's sister's boyfriend, Cliff, happened to be in the nightclub that evening and came to my mother's aid. In the chaos, my father pulled a gun on my mother and Cliff. They backed down and my father fled because it was violation of his parole to drink, do drugs, or possess a gun.

Panicked, my mother rushed to her car, only to find the headlights and windows smashed. Our father had told her many times that if he couldn't have her, no one could. After he pulled a gun on her, she no longer believed this was an idle threat. He was a dangerous drug addict. Now she was terrified—for my brother and me. With no time to worry about her car, she raced home to make sure my father hadn't attempted to kidnap or harm her boys. We were safe, but her fear that night shook me badly.

Not long after that, my mother did the only thing she could do: she packed up everything we owned and moved our family to Kansas City, Missouri. She knew she needed to get us away from our father and Des Moines. She could no longer stay with a man whose first and only love was getting high.

A new life lay ahead whether I liked it or not. Being an optimist, my mind and focus quickly shifted toward the hope of greener pastures. But this attempt to create a better life would only become a nightmare.

CHAPTER 3

KANSAS CITY HERE I COME

My mother's younger sister, Kathryn (my Aunt Kate), lived in Kansas City with her husband and three children. Up to that point, I couldn't really remember ever meeting Aunt Kate's kids or her husband. I vaguely remembered her. For all intents and purposes, they were strangers.

As we pulled the beat-up station wagon and packed U-Haul trailer into the community where Aunt Kate lived, I couldn't believe its beauty. The houses were the nicest I'd ever seen. An immediate sense of insecurity filled me; we had no business being in a neighborhood with such majesty. We made a right turn into the driveway that led to their home, a stunning, single-story brick ranch-style house. I had no idea anyone we knew lived in a place like this. Now it would be our temporary home until my mother could get on her feet.

Upon entering the house, I struggled to take in the beauty I saw. The foyer had a marble floor with a gold chandelier. Each room was decorated in a different motif and color. Everything, from the furniture to the carpet, was pristine. I didn't dare touch anything or sit down for fear that I would damage something my mother could not afford to replace. If this was any indication of how life in Kansas City was going to be, things were definitely looking up.

Aunt Kate had married an affluent businessman. His father was not only a pioneer of a black-owned business in the city; he was one of the most successful black entrepreneurs in the United States. He'd started his business selling ethnic hair care products and cosmetics out of the trunk of his car in the mid-1940s and turned it into a multimillion-dollar distributorship. His son grew up in the business and after graduating from college ran the day-to-day operations before eventually taking over the company. Like his father before him, he was incredibly successful.

While standing in the foyer of their beautiful home, a fair-skinned African-American man of average height and with a strong build came to greet us. He hugged my mother. Then, he turned to Montez and me and with his million dollar smile said, "Hello nephews," as he reached out to shake our hands. It was Aunt Kate's husband, G. Lawrence Blankinship Jr.—my uncle.

He was the most handsome, well-groomed man I'd ever met. His appearance was impeccable. His beard and haircut were works of art. The shirt that he was wearing was flawlessly pressed with his initials "GLB" monogrammed on the cuffs. There was something different about him; I could sense I was in the presence of someone important.

Every morning he would drive himself to work in a beautiful, late model Buick Riviera. I had never met anyone so distinguished, well spoken, and with such a commanding presence. From the beginning, I idolized Uncle Lawrence. He was an African-American business icon and was only in his early 20s.

He was well educated, mature, and had the work ethic of a colony of ants. He put in twelve-hour workdays, seven days a week—something I would learn to emulate. But the thing I most admired about him was that he was rich. He always carried a money clip loaded with $100, $50 and $20 bills. He never seemed to run out of big bills. It didn't take me long to decide that I wanted to be exactly like him when I grew up.

Uncle Lawrence and I really hit it off. Maybe it was because I was the oldest of all the kids. Maybe it was because he saw some of himself in me. Maybe it was because whatever he valued, I learned to value. I saw how important hard work was to him, so I worked hard to get his attention and approval. Over the next nine years I would spend more time with him than anyone, even his own children. He would be the closest thing I would ever have to a father much to the chagrin of Aunt Kate.

A Bitter Christmas

Living with the Blankinships was an awakening of sorts. They lived a life of privilege and were influential within the community. Uncle Lawrence was highly sought after for his opinions on running a successful black-owned business. He graced the pages of Black Enterprise and Jet magazines. It felt like I was living The Fresh Prince of Bel-Air.

However, we were always on the outside looking in at their seemingly perfect life. The Blankinship family was very different from ours. They didn't have the same struggles my mother, brother and I had. They seemed to live an ideal existence. I found myself comparing their family and financial situation to ours, and it left me feeling intensely inferior. It felt as though we had been invited inside their lifestyle but only as spectators. We could watch but never engage. We didn't really belong, and the more I saw how my aunt and uncle lived, the more desperately I coveted what they had.

The first order of business upon arriving in Kansas City was getting Montez and me enrolled in school. I began fourth grade at Eastwood Hills Elementary School. Soon after, my mom found work in a small fast food restaurant called The Windmill on 71st Street and Prospect Avenue. Aunt Kate had made it clear to my mother that we were temporary guests in her home, and mom had a short window of time to establish herself.

Just before Christmas, we moved into our own apartment—the first and nicest place we would occupy in Kansas City. It was a two-bedroom with a Hollywood bath on the south side of the city off of Blue Ridge and Bannister Roads. We didn't have much in that apartment: our beds, a sofa, TV, and a stereo that we would use daily to play music from the likes of Lakeside, Teddy Pendergrass, and Maze featuring Frankie Beverly. The apartment was clean and in a decent neighborhood, and it was ours. Little did I know at the time, but that would be the best things would be for us in Kansas City. Our living standard would decline precipitously in the years ahead.

But at that time, I had high hopes. Christmas of 1980 was approaching fast and I had faith that it would be a good one, even though I knew our family was struggling financially. My mother had given up a good job in Des Moines to get us away from our father, so money was tight. Still, I think all children wish for their favorite toys on Christmas and I was no different. I had hope, even though I knew my mother was the real Santa Claus. However, when my brother and I rose at dawn on that cold, snowy Christmas morning and crept into the living room to find our gifts, our excitement vanished. There was no tree, no gifts, no nothing. We couldn't understand what had happened. With our heads hanging low, we tiptoed back into our bedroom, careful not to wake our sleeping mother, and lay in our beds with tears in our eyes. We must have done something really bad, I thought. We had to be the only kids in the world who wouldn't be opening presents on Christmas day.

About an hour later a voice said, "Frank!" It was my mother. I jumped up from my bed in a split second because mom was a strict disciplinarian, and anytime she called our names we were expected to come to her immediately. I also couldn't help but think she was about to deliver the news that Christmas had been saved after all.

When I got to the living room, she sat lifeless on the sofa in her bathrobe.

"Yes, Mom?" She reached out her hand.

"Here. Take this and buy something for you and your brother for Christmas."

It was a five-dollar bill. My anticipation turned to disappointment. Five dollars! I thought. What in the heck am I going to buy with five dollars? Even in 1980 five dollars didn't buy much.

Numb, I went back to the bedroom where Montez was awaiting my return. "What'd she say?" he asked. I showed him the tattered five-dollar bill and his face fell. My fourth grade math skills quickly told me that we each had $2.50 to spend.

We got dressed, walked to the nearby neighborhood grocery store and immediately found the aisle that housed a small collection of toys and began to scour the meager selection. The best toys all cost more than $2.50, and there was no way we were going to share a gift. We both wanted our own present. So that Christmas, we each became the proud owner of matching dart guns. We walked home from the grocery store that cold and snowy morning playing cops and robbers.

Later that morning, I was struck by an overwhelming sense of guilt. I had acted ungratefully when my mother handed me the five-dollar bill. Maybe Montez and I didn't have a Christmas tree or any of the gifts we wanted, but at least we got something. I felt terrible. I wanted to give my mother a hug and a kiss to let her know that I was grateful and that I loved her.

I ran out to the living room and startled her as I entered. I saw something

I had never seen before. My mother was smoking something that looked like a cigarette, but I knew that smell. It was a joint. I stopped in my tracks and stared. I was embarrassed because I felt as if I'd intruded on her.

I knew my mother smoked weed. She had been doing it ever since I could remember, and she always tried to hide it from us. But I was no dummy. We'd find marijuana seeds and roaches in ashtrays all the time. But I had never caught her in the act. She looked at me with a ferocious scowl and said, "Don't you say anything to anybody!" Without saying a word, I turned around, ran to my room, jumped into my bed and began to sob.

I wasn't upset because I had caught my mother smoking weed. I wasn't even upset at being scolded to keep my little mouth shut. I was upset because it was Christmas and all my little brother and I got was five dollars to buy two cheap dart guns from a grocery store. While my mother had enough money to buy drugs and alcohol daily, she didn't have enough to buy us anything for Christmas. She had begun to choose her addictions over us.

Double Dipping

From that day on, we survived by any means necessary. The worse our situation got, the more disreputable our survival tactics became. Kansas City had a higher cost of living than Des Moines and my mother was making less money. In order to supplement her minimum wage job, she also collected welfare from the state of Iowa. We were double dipping. The welfare benefits were supposed to be our life preserver, keeping us afloat only until we could make it on our own. But that day never came.

Every month, we would drive to Des Moines to pick up our welfare check and food stamps. Montez and I would always get excited about making the trip. The possibility of getting to see family we left behind—especially our cousins—thrilled us. But we rarely saw anyone, because we often left Kansas City late at night in stealth mode. My mother was a private person and didn't want anybody knowing her business.

We would load up the car with snacks and soda and a cooler full of beer for my mom. These trips were one of the few times that I actually connected with my mother. I was her co-pilot. We'd play music the whole time and sing along to the lyrics of our favorite songs. No matter how bad our circumstances were, it was one of the pleasures I enjoyed most. However, several times every trip, my mom would pull over at a public rest area to take a break, and she would always park as far as she could from the restrooms and the lights, even when it was cold and snowy outside.

In the pitch dark and in the middle of no-man's land, she would always make us get out of the car to use the restroom, even if we were sound asleep. The three of us would run together to the restrooms; Montez and I, knowing that we were our mother's knight protectors, stayed with her and stayed together.

Once we arrived back at the car to continue our journey, my mother would bark, "Go run! Stretch your legs some more!" This was not a suggestion. My mother didn't make suggestions. She gave orders and they were not subject to negotiation. So we would run around for five or ten minutes in the dark, sometimes in the snow. Finally, she would flash the high beam headlights; our cue to race back to the car. When we got back in, there was always the stench of marijuana. But we didn't dare say a word. She would repeat this charade at every rest stop.

These late night road trips to Des Moines were always quick. We would spend three hours driving there and no more than two hours in the city. No sooner would my mother pick up her check and food stamps and we'd be back on the road home. The trips were not about socializing. They were about getting in and out as quickly as possible and being seen by as few people as possible—especially my dad. But the trips were torture for us. We missed our cousins and our old friends. We would have loved to spend time with them.

With each passing month, life got harder. Despite my mother working and collecting welfare, there was never enough money. Meanwhile, my mother's drinking and drug use intensified. I was discovering the maxim "wherever you go, there you are". We had moved to Kansas City, but we had brought our troubles from Des Moines with us in that U-Haul trailer.

Thief

Poverty is about more than just not having things. It grinds you down emotionally. The desperation of poverty breeds bad choices. It did that to me, and having lived with the Blankinships and seen what their life was like, the stark contrast made our poverty even more unbearable. Finally, I decided to do something about it.

During the spring of my fourth grade year I noticed that most kids kept their lunch money in their pencil boxes. One day I decided that I wanted every kid's lunch money for myself. That morning during recess, as soon as I saw that everyone was busy playing and the teachers were distracted, I slipped back into the unlocked door of our classroom. I ransacked every desk for any trace of cash. Then, as I made my way toward the door, I saw the mother lode: the teacher's desk.

Curiosity got the best of me. I rummaged through the desk and saw several dollar bills. I picked them up and stashed them in my already full pockets. I had hit the jackpot.

Suddenly, I spotted someone walking down the hall just outside the classroom. Panicked, I slammed the teacher's desk drawer shut and ran to the one-person bathroom in the back of the classroom to hide. The sound of the desk drawer slamming shut must have alerted the passerby, because they came into the classroom to investigate. As I stood in the dark breathing hard with fear, the door to the bathroom opened. It was one of the other teachers from a neighboring class. She stared down at me. She knew I was up to something. After she asked me repeatedly what I was doing, I broke down and confessed.

"I'm sorry. Please don't call my mother. Please." The teacher dragged me down the hall to the principal's office, where my mother was called immediately. While the principal spoke with her, I grew terrified of what my mother was going to do. Then the principal handed me the phone. My mother wanted to speak with me. "Wait until you get home," she said with a hiss. I felt every tick of the clock the rest of that school day. I did not want to go home. I knew I was going to pay for what I had done.

When we arrived home from school, my mother ordered my brother into the bedroom. "Get the belt," she said to me. Silently, I retrieved the belt and handed it to her. I knew we were past talking. She began to hurl the leather belt with the kind of vehemence that can only come from years of experience on the receiving end of a beating. She beat me until I could barely walk—until she felt that I had gotten the message. However, our poverty would continue to speak louder to me than the consequences of a physical thrashing.

School Clothes

As our usual "home alone" summer came to a close, I was excited about the start of the new school year. I would be a fifth grader and starting at a new school, Westridge Elementary. Every year, the start of school brought the anticipation of new clothes and new shoes. It was as if the first two weeks of school were a fashion show. Every kid looked forward to showing off his or her new clothes with pride. Montez and I were no different. We couldn't wait to go shopping for new gear to show off and have us feeling our best.

On the last weekend before the start of school, we were eager for the shopping trip to buy our new clothes. But Saturday flew by; no shopping trip. There was something wrong. We could feel it.

That Sunday, we waited anxiously for the words, "Let's go shopping." But by six o'clock in the evening, the mall had closed. There would be no new clothes or shoes for us on the first day of school. I didn't know what was going on, but I knew that we would probably be the only kids who didn't have new clothes and shoes the next day. I felt ashamed knowing we'd be wearing the same worn-out pants, shirts and shoes from the year before.

The next morning, as we got ourselves ready for school, my mother stopped us. "You're not going to school today," she said. "Tonight, when I get home from work, I'll take you shopping for school clothes." Relief washed over me. She knew, just as we did, how humiliating it would be for us to show up at school with old, faded clothes. My mother went off to work that morning and Montez and I had one additional day of lockdown.

However, when she returned that evening, she said nothing about shopping. Neither of us had the nerve to ask about it. Surely, she hadn't forgotten. The next morning, she informed us again that we were not going to school. "One more day," my mother stated. "I promise we'll go school shopping tonight. I promise." Thank God. Again, Montez and I sat at home all day watching the clock, anticipating my mother's return from work. But when she got home, she barely spoke to us. The night would come and go with no trip to the mall.

I knew my mom was feeling the pressure of not being able to provide for us the way she would have liked. She had been the kid too poor for new clothes, and she didn't want us to be those kids. Her self-esteem was pushing her to provide for us in a way she didn't have the means to do. "Don't worry. We're going to get your clothes this weekend," she promised.

We missed the entire first week of school because we didn't have new clothes. I hoped that she would keep her word and take us shopping on the weekend. But I wasn't sure I could trust her word.

Even so, from the time we woke on that Saturday morning, the focus of every waking second was our trip to the mall. School clothes were the elephant in the room, the taboo subject. But Saturday came and went. Then Sunday came and went. Nothing. We had already missed the entire first week of school.

I can't imagine how this must have crushed my mother's fragile sense of pride. We knew she loved us. She wanted nothing more than to meet our every need. But, she was a facing a harsh reality: we weren't making it. She wanted her words to change things, but of course they didn't.

We finally started school on the first day of the third week with the same clothes and shoes we'd worn the previous year. I could feel my mother's despair. She was one step closer to complete surrender.

CHAPTER 4

3538 GARFIELD

Our first apartment in Kansas City was respectable, but our financial condition continued to deteriorate and we could no longer afford it. Something had to change or we were eventually going to be staring at an eviction notice. Fortunately, my mother had befriended one of her co-workers, a young woman named Chattie. After hearing of our struggles, Chattie was kind enough to help.

She invited us to live with her and her young daughter in their small apartment on The Paseo, a wide boulevard that, thirty years earlier, had been one of the classiest streets in Kansas City. My brother and I weren't excited about losing our own space, but my mother never consulted us on the matter.

Chattie was a character. She had a dark ebony complexion, a thick Southern accent and a larger than life personality. She spoke so loudly it was as though she was deaf. But her most unmistakable features were her Jheri curl and the gold cap she wore on her upper middle tooth. Whenever she spoke, my brother and I would fall on the floor laughing.

Living with Chattie wasn't ideal. Her apartment was small, and we had no bedroom. Montez and I slept in the middle of the living room floor using sheets and blankets as makeshift beds while my mother slept on the sofa. The building was so old that heat came from a central boiler system and a radiator, which meant we were always cold that winter. But we made do. That was just what we did.

Late one night, after my brother and I had already been asleep for quite a while, my mother entered the living room. I felt a nudge on my shoulder and her gentle whisper say, "Frank. Montez. Wake up. Get up and get dressed."

Half asleep, I said, "Huh?"

My mother, in a low, forceful tone: "Frank and Montez, get up! Put your clothes and shoes on, and pack your stuff up."

Groggy and half asleep, we did as our mother instructed as she began to gather her things and ours.

Suddenly, out of the darkness, Chattie entered and sat in a chair on the far side of the living room. She didn't say a word. She just stared. But if her facial expression could've spoken, the words would have been loud, violent, and angry. My mother said nothing. I could feel the tension, and I began packing a little more quickly.

We made our way down the stairs of the building to the street and our midnight blue, 1971 Plymouth Satellite. In the cold of winter, we loaded our things and drove off. Silence. My brother lay in the back seat and fell asleep. I sat in the front seat with my mother, cold and exhausted, dozing off and waking up.

We drove around the dark, empty streets of Kansas City for a while, and it slowly dawned on me that we had no place to go. It was so quiet in the car that I could almost hear my mother thinking. Finally, we came to the parking lot of a city park. My mother backed the car into a space so that we could see anyone who might unexpectedly pull into the lot. Our car came to a complete stop but the engine continued to idle as the heat blasted full throttle in an attempt to keep the freezing night air out.

There we were sleeping in a car in the middle of winter with no place to go. Why didn't my mother call her sister? Was it pride? Or was calling her sister not an option? I could only guess at that point, because my mother wasn't exactly sharing her thoughts with my brother and me. One thing was clear: Kansas City had become a nightmare. We lived in a world of uncertainty, not knowing where we were going to lay our heads from night to night. Our insecurity kept me fearful.

Visitors Again

With no backup plan, my mother was forced to humble herself and call her friend Anna. Anna was a white woman married to an African-American man, Bobby, who my mother knew from Des Moines. Fortunately for us, Anna was sympathetic to our situation. Anna, Bobby, and Anna's son, Michael, had a nice home in the middle-class community of Hickman Mills. They welcomed us into their home until my mother could get back on her feet.

I was terrified at the prospect of living with yet another family. What if they decided to throw us out too? Where would we go? I didn't know whether my mother was trying to hide or trying to keep us from seeing the reality that we were sliding deeper into poverty and running through safety nets quicker than we could establish new ones.

We lived with Anna, Bobby and Michael for several months, until my mother was able to scrape together some money and figure out what our next move would be. Bobby's stepmother, Carrie Bumpus, owned a house with several living units and she had one for rent. Bobby made the introduction and the apartment was ours. It was our fifth address in our two years in Kansas City, and we'd call it home for the next several years.

The apartment was deep in the inner city, in the worst neighborhood we'd ever lived in. Signs of brokenness were all over the streets and the faces of the people who walked them. Vacant buildings, graffiti and drug use were visible everywhere. Police patrolled the streets continuously. Compared to the people who dwelt here, I was a sheltered suburban kid. I would have to adapt—to learn street skills and develop a primal, kill-or-be-killed attitude—to survive.

Our new landlord, Mrs. Bumpus, was a lively old southern lady who wore big Sally Jessy Raphael glasses. She was God-fearing and churchgoing, but she still liked to drink her beer. When she did, it wasn't unusual to see her outside in the yard, cursing her husband. She was Madea before Tyler Perry ever created the character. She was funny, witty and had a good sense of humor. When my mother would send Montez and me to deliver the monthly rent check, Mrs. Bumpus would always say, "Thankya Gee-zussss!" Apparently, she was elated to receive something, even if it was late.

With us, the rent usually was. When we were late, we'd try sneaking in and out of our apartment to avoid being questioned. But Mrs. Bumpus was nobody's fool. Sometimes, she'd wait for us to come strolling home after school and catch us before we could dodge her.

"When's your mother going to pay the rent?" she'd drawl. "It's late. Have your mother to call me," she'd say with her syrupy accent. Then she'd retreat into her house.

I hated that we were behind on our rent. But I hated more that I didn't have the ability to do anything about it. It sucked to be eleven years old and be the front man for a mother who was trying to hide from the world. But no matter how late the rent was Mrs. Bumpus never tried to evict us. She knew my mother was on welfare and was struggling. Of course, the squalid condition of our apartment probably had something to do with her compassion.

Losing the Rodent and Roach War

The space we rented at 3538 Garfield was a converted attic up four flights of stairs. The ceilings were low and vaulted at funky angles because the roof was, literally, on top of us. Our 650 square feet included one bedroom and one bathroom. The small living room doubled as my mother's bedroom. Even at its cleanest, the place was a dump.

By most people's standards, our living conditions would have been intolerable. Mrs. Bumpus let us stay because no one with any other options would have paid a dime for such a hovel. We had no such options, and we couldn't afford standards. We needed a roof over our heads.

But while living without proper heating and cooling or a refrigerator full of food was bearable, the pests made the place nearly unlivable. Roaches, mice, and rats had long since taken over. When the lights went out at night, we would hear the rodents scurrying in the kitchen in search of food. We had to be cautious when making a sandwich because it wasn't uncommon to find that mice had chewed through the bag and the bread. More than once, we poured out cereal to find a rodent still in the box. The constant scratching sounds would make my skin crawl.

I was always afraid that a rat or mouse would bite me and give me rabies, so Montez and I set traps in an attempt to eradicate them. It wasn't unusual for us to wake up in the middle of the night to the "pop" sound of a trap snapping shut. We'd get up, do the gruesome work of taking the bloody, twitching bodies off the traps, dispose of them and reset the traps. There were way too many of the foul creatures for us to kill them all. Sometimes, just seconds after we reset a trap, we'd hear the "snap" and squeal of another kill.

The rodents were only the half of it. Roaches had long since overwhelmed our little attic apartment. It was nothing to turn on the lights late at night and see hundreds or thousands of roaches all over the kitchen. We would spray, set mist bombs and use boric acid, but nothing worked. We couldn't even eat a meal without roaches climbing all over the place. They were in the refrigerator, the toaster, in cabinets on the clean dishes—everywhere. It wasn't surprising to be sleeping and feel a roach climbing on you. We'd wake in a panic, shaking our blankets and pajamas with a fury.

Our roach infestation was so vile it caused us problems outside of our home. We found out the hard way that roaches like to travel. It was impossible to keep them out of anything—food, clothes or furniture. Because my brother and I liked to escape our living conditions as often as we could by sleeping at the Blankinships, we had inadvertently transported roaches into their home. We didn't have a washer or dryer inside of our apartment or money to go to a laundromat, so we usually washed our clothes in the sink and dried them by the heat of the stove. But when we went to the Blankinship home, sometimes Montez and I would sneak a load of dirty clothes into their washer and dryer in order to save money or the pain of washing them by hand…and the roaches would come along for the ride.

Roaches like to lay eggs in warm places—like laundry baskets or piles of dirty clothes. Without knowing it, we'd infested the Blankinship house. Aunt Kate immediately blamed us because there was no way her home would ever have roaches unless we were hand delivering them. "Don't be bringing your clothes over here anymore," she scolded. Her angry rejection only made us feel worse.

Aunt Kate had a special knack for making me feel like a burden on her family's upper-class lifestyle. Despite her obvious contempt, for the most part I could handle her. But, in some ways, Uncle Lawrence made me feel worse. He was my hero, my idol. I was expecting him to save me from poverty. I held out hope that one day, he would adopt us and we'd get to live in their beautiful home.

On some level, I knew I was putting unrealistic expectations on him, but the little boy in me wanted to be saved by the only man who'd ever taken an interest in me. At that age, that's what I thought heroes did. But in all the years we lived in Kansas City—during the hundreds of times he picked me up or dropped me off—he never came inside our home. Not once. And it hurt me deeply. He knew the places we lived in were dumps; you didn't have to come inside to see that. I felt like he thought our poverty was a contagious disease. Or worse, if he saw how we really lived with his own eyes he would feel some responsibility to help change it. I always hoped one day, Uncle Lawrence would be my real life Superman and rescue us. But he never showed up for me in that way.

At eleven, I realized if we were ever going to get out of poverty, we were going to have to find our own way out. From my perspective, money was our problem, and money was the only answer.

The Passing of Aunt Jackie

As the months passed, our situation became more dire. My mother seemed to be slipping into a darker emotional state; her confidence and fight had faded. Nothing she did gave her any hope that we would escape our situation. She was trying her best, but every time she took one step forward, she'd end up taking ten steps backward. As a result, her drinking and drug use increased. The straw that broke her back finally fell on a cold winter day between Christmas 1982 and New Year's Day 1983.

Our modest Christmas had ended, thank God. Our financial desperation—and the impossible example of the prosperous and happy Blankinship family—had made me despise birthdays and holidays. The sharp contrast was just a reminder of how hopeless our lives were.

One morning after Christmas, as my brother and I played in our room, I heard the phone ring. We rarely answered the phone. My mother had become a recluse who didn't like talking on the phone. Few people, other than bill collectors or telemarketers, ever called us anyway. But this time, after several rings, my mother answered.

"Hello?" There was an elongated pause between my mother's gentle greeting and what I heard next. I focused on putting together the Legos that Montez and I loved to play with. But within seconds, a loud scream rose from the living room. It was the sound of a 1,000-pound grizzly with its paw caught in a trap. "Noooooooooooooooo!!!"

Startled and frightened, my brother and I dashed into the living room, where our mother lay on the floor in the fetal position, clutching the telephone, hysterical. We immediately got on the floor and clung to her and started to weep fearfully.

Seeing my mother like this, broken and helpless with anguish, was terrifying. She'd always been the strong-willed type who never showed emotion. After several minutes, she was able to pull herself together and continue the phone conversation. The news was devastating.

Her older sister, Jackie—my mother's rock, the sibling she was closest to—was dead at the age of 29. From the one-sided conversation I could hear, it sounded as if her death had been due to foul play. But quickly, the conversation turned to who would care for Jackie's three children. In heat of the circumstances, my mother vowed to care for her sister's kids, something she had no ability to do. She knew it. We knew it. Everyone knew it.

After hanging up the phone, my mother held us tightly. "I don't know what I would do if something happened to either of you," she said with tears in her eyes. "If something happened to either one of you, we'd all go together." With my childlike understanding, I felt the same. I couldn't imagine living without my mother or brother. Life was a constant struggle, but they were all I had. We were a team. And no matter how bad things got, I never questioned whether my mother loved us. We had what I thought was an unbreakable bond.

Nevertheless, the passing of my Aunt Jackie was a breaking point for my mother. It was a body blow only matched by her mother's death almost 15 years earlier. She hadn't had the opportunity to say goodbye to either of them. Her mother passed away while she was in foster care; she was the only child who wasn't present in the family home. Now her sister, whom she loved most out of all her siblings, was gone. And she never recovered from the loss.

CHAPTER 5

HUMILIATION

From that Christmas morning a couple of years earlier, when my brother and I received nothing from Santa Claus, all the problems my family faced seemed to have one simple answer: money. I didn't realize it, but I was willing to pay any price in order to get as much of it as I could.

Starting in 1983, I did whatever I could to make money. Early on, my source of income was cutting grass; Uncle Lawrence was my biggest customer. Every week I would cut his grass and he would pay me twenty dollars for my effort. He would also allow me to use his lawn mower to drum up other business in his neighborhood. The money I made gave me a healthy dose of pride. It afforded me the opportunity to buy gum, candy and other junk foods, but it also gave me the ability to help my mother buy gas or a bag of groceries.

I liked the way I felt when I had money in my pocket. I didn't feel as needy or helpless. I felt powerful. I learned the power of money from watching Uncle Lawrence. A lot of times after attending mass on Saturday afternoons, he would take all of us kids out to eat. In my family, we rarely, if ever, got to eat out. It was just too expensive. My mother had to stretch what little money we had. Being with Uncle Lawrence always gave me a tremendous sense of security. He seemed to have it all together and was highly respected in the community. If that's what money brought, I wanted it for myself.

So you can imagine how thrilled I was when, when I was eleven years old, Uncle Lawrence gave me my first real job. I worked in the warehouse of his distributorship, side-by-side with some of his other employees. I reported to the same location, at the same time, every day during the summer. I was paid an hourly wage. I was officially one of his employees, and I loved every part of it because I got the chance to make money and spend more time shadowing my uncle.

Working that first summer, I began to understand the power of being an hourly wage earner. I was being paid the federal minimum wage—$3.35 per hour—and I soon learned about the value of overtime pay. I found out that if I worked more than 40 hours in a workweek I would get paid time-and-a-half for the extra hours. That was $5 per hour! As a result, I worked every second of every day that I could. The warehouse manager literally had to send me home because I wouldn't leave. I was trying to make a million dollars every day because money—the lack of it—was the cancer that was destroying my family. My desire to make money and earn the admiration of my uncle created a high-octane drive that produced a relentless work ethic.

It wasn't difficult for me to work long hours, because my uncle was a workaholic. He would pick me up early in the morning and take me home late in the evening. That meant a minimum of 12 hours a day. Uncle Lawrence loved being a business owner, and that worked to my advantage.

However, Uncle Lawrence had high expectations for everyone who worked for him—me included. I worked as hard or harder than everyone there, even my uncle. If I came in to work and just did an average job, I would have set a bad example. So I did everything I could to be a model employee. I would continue to work for my uncle every summer until I finished high school in 1989.

With the income from my job, I felt rich. I didn't know anyone my age making the kind of money I was. Some adults I knew weren't making the kind of money I was making! Unfortunately, I also had a more stable job and income than my mother did. While she was struggling for stability, I had it working for my uncle. While I had a steady paycheck—at least for the summer—she was struggling to keep food on the table. That meant that nearly all the money I made was being used to provide for my family. Virtually every dollar I earned went to pay for food, rent, utilities or clothing. So as quickly as I was earning it, it was spent.

The most difficult part of working hard and having nothing tangible to show for it was watching my cousins (who were given jobs, too) save their money or buy things they wanted. They were seeing the fruits of their labor. I was breaking my back in the heat and humidity of the summer and seeing nothing in return for my hard work. My mother was taking everything. It was incredibly frustrating, and every summer it was the same thing. The burden of supporting our family had moved from my mother's shoulders to mine, and I watched as she slowly retreated from life.

Of course, when the summers came to an end, so did my paychecks. I still had to attend school. But my family had become dependent on the $800-900 a month I made during the summers, so come fall we were right back in a place of lack.

Swallowing My Pride

Many times when we fell short of cash (which was often), my mother would put me up to the task of asking Uncle Lawrence for help. I despised asking him for money. He was my idol. I wanted him to see me as strong and capable just like he was, not weak and needy. My mother knew how much I admired and respected him, and she knew he had taken a strong interest in my life. She knew he wouldn't deny me if I asked him for help. I didn't realize how manipulative this was until years later.

At first, I would ask for $30 or $40. But as things got worse, the amounts increased. Every time I asked, Uncle Lawrence always came through. However, each time I asked I felt like I lost a part of myself. It's one thing when strangers know you're losing at life. It's another thing to have to look someone in the eyes who you respect dearly and beg for help. In those situations, I would always freeze up. My eyes would drop to the floor and I would have to push the words past my pride. Afterwards, there was a part of me that never wanted to see him again. I'm sure it made him just as uncomfortable to have me begging him for money.

One summer morning, as I prepared for work, my mother instructed me to ask Uncle Lawrence for financial help. Queasiness overcame me. As I waited for Uncle Lawrence to pick me up, I dreaded seeing him. When he showed up and I got into his car, I greeted him with a distant, "Good morning." He replied like he did each day, "Good morning nephew." Immediately, an awkward silence filled his Lincoln Town Car. I felt flushed with shame and the guilt of having to ask him for help yet again. There was no way I was going to be able to ask him on the ride to work. I couldn't muster the courage. I decided to wait until later that evening after everyone in the office was gone.

That day was miserable. When night fell and we were the only two remaining in the building, I walked into his office and sat across from him at his desk. My emotions overcame me, and I broke down sobbing.

Shocked by my outburst, he asked, "What's wrong?" Choking on tears, I couldn't speak. But he knew what the problem was immediately.

Without another word, he opened the drawer of his large, cluttered executive desk, pulled out his checkbook and wrote me a check for $500. Then he stood, reached into his pocket, and pulled out his money clip. He peeled off five $100 bills, held them up and said, "Do you see this?" Feeling worthless and completely vulnerable, all I could manage was a nod.

He proceeded to the bookcase in his office and grabbed a book off the shelf. "This is the encyclopedia letter 'F' for Frank," he said. "I'm putting this $500 here. If you ever need anything, you come in here and you get what you need." I could tell he was upset, but not with me. He was angry with my mother for sending a child to do something she should have had the courage to do herself.

"There will always be $500 here, no matter what you take. Do you understand me?" he asked. I nodded and tears streamed down my face. His generosity overwhelmed me, but it humiliated me at the same time. I didn't think I would ever be able to look him in the eyes again. From that day, I felt like no matter how successful I might become, I had lost a piece of myself to him. It caused me to career from one emotional guardrail (extreme need) to another (extreme self-reliance).

That day, I made a decision that would cause me more harm than any choice I have ever made: I decided I would never ask for anyone's help ever again. I would do whatever I had to do in order to get what I needed on my own.

Months later I went into Uncle Lawrence's office when no one was around. I didn't need anything. I just wanted to look at the $500 and know that I was taken care of, secure. I grabbed the encyclopedia letter "F" and flipped through the pages. The money was gone. I felt sickened. Uncle Lawrence didn't owe me anything; everything he did was out of kindness. Opening that encyclopedia and seeing nothing in it made me feel like a beggar who Uncle Lawrence took pity on because he couldn't say no.

Another New School

Uncle Lawrence despised the fact that my mother would put me up to the task of asking him for money. So did Aunt Kate. But she wasn't as diplomatic as her husband. She seethed with anger that my mother would take advantage of him. With my mother in hiding from the world, my brother and I were the targets of her anger.

When my mom owed her money, Aunt Kate would make sure Montez and I knew about it. She would say, "Your mom owes money. Ask her when she's going to pay me." She knew there was nothing we could do about it, yet, she chose to burden us because she couldn't get to my mother. While Uncle Lawrence was trying to build me up, Aunt Kate was cutting me off at the knees. She could be cold, callous and vengeful. It was hard to love her when she was always attacking me for her sister's failures.

That following year, our decline worsened. Aunt Kate was growing bitter and resentful of the stress my mother placed on her and her family. Her acrimony toward my mother manifested itself in ways that were mean and heartless. It wasn't uncommon for her to deny us entry into her home after school or make us leave. There were times when we would be at her home after school and she'd be cooking dinner. If I even hinted that I liked the smell of what she was cooking she'd say, "There's not enough for you."

Montez and I would head for home, cursing her for how she treated us. Her words and actions were downright evil. She couldn't express her anger to our mother face-to-face, so she was hurting her through her helpless children. After my sixth grade year, Aunt Kate forbade us from using the Blankinship family address to attend school in their district. This prohibition would mean I would be attending my fourth school in four years in Kansas City.

My fourth school would be Central Junior High, one of the worst performing and most chaotic schools in the city. I was used to going to schools with positive and upbeat environments where learning and achievement were encouraged. Central was the antithesis of that. It was a dark, old, rundown building resembling a prison. The school had steel mesh grates that covered the windows to keep people from vandalizing it. A tall, stocky African-American security guard patrolled the grounds to discourage fighting, skipping class, drug use and dealing, having sex, trespassing and loitering on school property.

I quickly realized that the inmates ran the asylum at Central Junior High. Many of the students—99 percent of whom were African-American—had no discipline, and the teachers didn't seem to care. Worst of all, our lessons were things I had learned two years earlier in the higher rated Raytown suburban school district. This made me a genius in my classes. But it didn't make me popular. My classmates would make fun of me for speaking proper English. "You talk like a white boy!" one kid said to me in front of the entire class; everyone laughed. It became a running joke. He mocked me by acting like an uppity, well-spoken, white snob. Every time he did it I would laugh, too, like it didn't bother me. It did, but I didn't want to become a lightning rod for his or some other insecure character's abuse.

Because of this taunting, I shut my mouth and tried to blend in. I let my test scores talk for me. That year I was inducted into the National Junior Honor Society. The school made a big fuss out of it because I don't think it happened too often. Uncle Lawrence made an appearance at the awards ceremony, and for that morning I felt like a son who had made his father proud.

Attending Central Junior High made it clear that I was different from the African-American kids in the Raytown suburban school district. I was fighting poverty every day, something most of them couldn't identify with. At the same time, I didn't fit in with the African-Americans kids in my own neighborhood either. I was teased for wanting to be educated and smart like my Uncle Lawrence. My peers told me that I was too "white"—not cool enough, a sellout. In seventh grade, it became clear that I didn't fit in either world. But given the choice of the two worlds, the suburban, white school district was where I felt most comfortable, and a game-changer was on the horizon.

One day in the middle of spring, while sitting in class, there was a "Pop! Pop!" sound that rang throughout the school. We were immediately put on lockdown for fear that someone was running around campus with a gun. Officials searched the school grounds, and outside the window of a first floor classroom they found a young boy bleeding from a gunshot wound.

Later, I would learn that there had been an altercation between two boys and one of them pulled out a .22 caliber handgun and shot the other in the mouth at point-blank range. Thank God, the boy lived. However, after that year, Uncle Lawrence would no longer allow me to go that school. He ordered Aunt Kate to get Montez and me out of the Kansas City Public Schools District. We would again be allowed to use the Blankinships' address. That put me in my uncle's debt again, but it also meant attending school in the calm and safety of the suburbs, which was worth it.

CHAPTER 6

HIGH SCHOOL BLUES

By the time I reached high school, my mother was no longer engaged in anything resembling employment. Worse, she was also suffering from what I now recognize as clinical depression. Dejected over her inability to provide for my brother and me, her casual drug and alcohol use had escalated to the point where sobriety was the exception and intoxication was the norm. By this time she was living with her boyfriend, a man that Montez and I had never even met, while we were left to fend for ourselves.

Her daily parenting check-in phone calls slowly turned into every other day, then every now and then. We saw her in person perhaps once or twice a week, and even that would decrease over the next year or two. I didn't understand why she would leave us by ourselves with little food or money. I guess I couldn't blame her for choosing to live at her boyfriend's home; I just assumed his place had to be better than our dump. Given the opportunity to live in a nicer, cleaner home, I would have done the same. Instead, I had the freedom that every teenage kid desired. For all intents and purposes, my brother and I were living on our own.

However, we were still expected to behave responsibly. My mother wasn't around often enough to physically discipline us, but her words were enough. She didn't accept excuses. So Montez and I would still rise every day and make the long trek from our downtrodden neighborhood to the Blankinship home and their nice suburban schools. We didn't want to feel our mother's wrath for breaking the rules, even if she wasn't around often enough to enforce them.

In high school, I felt that I was trapped between two worlds. The first was the world of my middle-to-upper-class high school peers and their families. The second was the world of poverty and despair that was my reality. The glaring difference between the two was torturous. My desire to fit in with my peers, who were living what I deemed "the good life," only kept me trying to keep up with the Joneses. The more I tried the more I realized how impossible it was. My only hope for sanity was divine intervention.

Thank goodness for Uncle Lawrence. He knew the Lord. He was a devout Catholic and weekly worship was a priority, no matter how hectic his business life was. Every Saturday afternoon, he made all five of us kids attend mass whether we liked it or not. By the time I was in high school I had been baptized, had my first holy communion and served as an altar boy but I had never read one word of the Bible. I had the ritual down but I didn't know the Lord.

Thank God, He knew me.

The day was quickly approaching the name of the Lord would be the only name remaining I could call on to save me from the perils of my fallen life.

Freshman Year 1985-1986

I entered my freshman year at Raytown South High School in the fall of 1985 as a fragile 14-year-old. I was excited about being in high school and beginning a new chapter in life. However, the kids were older and bigger, and many of the material requirements that determined popularity were out of reach for me.

I didn't have the expensive designer clothes to help build my self-esteem, and I was afraid to be exposed as a "district cheat." I was terrified that the gap between me and the other kids was too wide for me to matriculate into the mainstream and be seen as a normal kid. Sports became the solution to my freshman feelings of alienation.

My brother and I had always wanted to play sports. However, my mother wouldn't allow it. She claimed she feared that we would get hurt, but it had less to do with my mother's concern for our safety and more to do with her inability to pay for our involvement. We were barely getting by, so spending money on football equipment or basketball shoes was out of the question. So when the opportunity arose for me to play sports in high school, I was all over it. I could have weighed 50 pounds with Forrest Gump braces on my legs; I didn't care. I was going to play ball.

I was five feet eight inches and weighed 95 pounds. I wasn't the biggest kid in the world but what I lacked in brawn I made up for in heart. I had childhood dreams of playing in the National Football League (NFL) as a wide receiver like past stars Lynn Swann, Drew Pearson, or tight end, Kellen Winslow. The school district provided everything I needed except an athletic supporter and cleats, and with the money I made working for my Uncle Lawrence, I could take care of those myself. Transportation, however, would be a problem. Because my mother didn't have a reliable car or money for gas she was unable to support my athletics. And even if she had been able to use her boyfriend's car every day, she wasn't about to drive halfway across the city to pick me up from practice. It just wasn't feasible. Aunt Kate was not an option either. She'd made it very clear that she was not going to spend her precious time picking up a kid she resented.

Thank God for the Childress family. They were backyard neighbors of the Blankinships, and their oldest son, David, was a freshman, too. I'd known David ever since we moved to Kansas City; we'd played basketball and kickball together whenever I hung out at the Blankinship home. He had attended private parochial grade schools until the sixth grade, so I didn't really get to know him well. But when high school started and he went out for the football team, our friendship began to blossom.

David's parents would pick him up from practice and they were fine with me hitching a ride home with them. They also knew my brother and I didn't live in the school district, but it didn't seem to bother them much. If not for the Childress family, I would not have had the opportunity to play high school sports. They made possible a crucial part of life that helped shape and develop my character as a young man. For that I will always be thankful for them. But my relationship with the Childress family was only beginning.

Turnover

Freshman football was fun. Neither David nor I was a starter and leading up to the end of the season we had never played in a game. We weren't as big, fast, and strong as some of the other kids, and if you couldn't help the team win, you didn't play. But I didn't care. I was just happy to be a part of the team and have the opportunity to run, throw, catch and tackle—even if it was only in practice. I vowed to practice hard, study the playbook, and make the coaches notice my tenacity and preparation.

By the last game of the season, my hard work and diligence had paid off. Coach Breckenridge told me to be prepared because I might get a chance to play at quarterback. I had been put at the quarterback position several weeks prior because I just didn't have the breakaway speed to be a receiver. The week leading up to the game I studied my playbook and practiced harder than I ever did anything in my life. In the hopes that I might see the field, I asked Uncle Lawrence if he would come. He said he would try but I knew it was a long shot. By now I knew only a major emergency could draw him away from work.

During the game I kept nervously searching the bleachers for any sign of Uncle Lawrence. As anxious as I was about performing in front of him, I was more fearful of the prospect that he would show up and I'd not be given the opportunity to play in the game. Even though the coach said be ready, it was the last game of the season, and I hadn't played the entire year. There was no guarantee.

Suddenly, I spotted Uncle Lawrence sitting in the third or fourth row. Adrenaline shot through me. Now, there was only one problem. I needed to get into the game. I wanted to make him proud. I immediately glued myself to the coach's side. I would have done anything to get the chance to play that day. The precious minutes on the clock ticked away. Then, in the fourth quarter when I thought all was lost, out of nowhere, Coach Breckenridge yelled, "Thomas! Thomas! You're in!" I strapped my helmet on and received the play. Practically dizzy from adrenaline and with play call in hand, I dashed off to the huddle.

In the middle of the huddle, down on one knee, I barked, "Okay guys. I-right, 98-out on one. I-right, 98-out on one. Ready?"

"Break!" we shouted in unison and ran to our positions. I ran up to center and got the line set.

"Ready? Set! Hut!" I shouted with authority. The ball was snapped into my hands. I took a quick drop, rolled right and delivered the ball to an open wide receiver, Derrick Alexander, on the right sideline for a small gain and first down. My nervousness quickly turned into exhilaration.

In came the next play from the sideline. We broke the huddle and lined up in our formation. On the snap count, the ball hit my hands. The play's primary read was a split end post pattern. I took a five-step drop and had eyes only for my primary receiver. I was going for the touchdown no matter what the defense was. I wound up, and as my arm went forward to release the ball, a blitzing linebacker hit me in the ribcage. The ball fluttered out of my hand like a dead duck and the safety plucked it out of the air for an interception.

I walked off the field; head low, holding my ribs. The pain was the least of my concerns. I failed my team and, most importantly, I failed in front of the one man who I cared to impress more than any other person in the world. I felt like a loser.

Wrestler

That season, one of the assistant freshman football coaches, Ethan Hauck, had been hired as the head wrestling coach at Raytown South. Either he saw something in me during the freshman football season or he was simply trying to get more boys to go out for the team, because he told me he thought I would make a good wrestler.

The only wrestling I knew at the time was what I watched on TV. Characters like Rick Flair and Andre the Giant were two of the biggest names in the sport. I loved watching as a kid but I had no interest in getting hit in the head with folding metal chairs and bleeding. Coach Hauck was persistent, though. I would pass by his classroom each day, and every time he'd ask if I was going to try out for the team. After about two weeks of this, I gave in. I didn't really want to. I just wanted him to quit pestering me. I didn't see myself as a wrestler. And since I didn't have transportation to get home after practice, I figured that would give me an easy way to get out of it. Then I found out that Coach had convinced David to try out for the team too. Now, I had no excuses because I knew David's parents would allow me to ride home with them.

At the beginning, I hated wrestling. I had no experience. I didn't know any moves, and I knew nothing about the sport. Most of the other guys on the team had been dedicated to the sport since elementary school. So early on I was always getting my butt kicked. But the competitor in me dug in and I began to learn a few moves. Before I knew it, I was beginning to give the more experienced guys an honest fight. They weren't taking me down like a ragdoll anymore, and by the end of the season I had earned my varsity letter and had become a pretty solid wrestler.

Wrestling, little did I know at the time, would become the cornerstone of my life and identity. It would also be the glue that cemented my relationship with David and the Childress family. David and I became best friends. We were inseparable. As our friendship evolved, I learned that I could trust him with my secrets and didn't have to hide who I was around him. His friendship toward me was built on who I was, not where I lived or my family's socioeconomic status. My friendship with David allowed me to be myself with someone at a time when I had more secrets than friends. My friendship with him and his parents quite possibly saved my life during some of the darkest times I would come up against during that period.

I credit the Childress family for many of the wonderful experiences I had in high school. Without their generosity and compassion, I wouldn't have competed as a wrestler or played one down of football. Sports opened the door for me to meet this fantastic family. David's parents, Chuck and Cheryl, were very supportive of him and I would be a direct beneficiary of that same support. During high school they became my surrogate parents—so much so that I called them "Moms" and "Pops". My mother was fading out and Cheryl was fading in. "Pops," on the other hand, was the closest I ever came to calling someone dad. They both rooted for me as enthusiastically as they rooted for their son and it felt good even if they weren't really my parents.

The work ethic that sports honed in me inspired me to challenge myself academically, too. With a newfound drive to be my best, I decided to challenge myself to see if I could earn straight As. Every day I would come home, study and do my homework no matter how tired I was, even after a grueling practice. I learned through sports that the body will quit long before the mind does. I was able to push myself farther than I ever had before.

When the third quarter of my freshman year was complete, I had earned seven As or A-minuses and one B-plus in French. I was proud that my freshman year had been a successful one. But more important, I learned that I had a power deep within me that I could tap to put my body and feelings in submission to my will.

Sophomore Year: 1986-1987

As the summer of 1986 was coming to a close, I was getting excited for my sophomore year and the upcoming football season. After that interception in the final game of my freshman campaign, I had something to prove to my teammates, my coaches and (mainly) myself. I had grown three inches and packed on 15 pounds of muscle since I started high school. My work ethic was impeccable, and in my mind I was ready to compete for a starting position. Unfortunately, before sophomore camp opened, David informed me that he didn't intend on playing football anymore. It was just not his game. I understood that. However, now I had no ride. I had no choice but to hang up my cleats. I told myself that I was just going to be a practice dummy for the better kids, and that quitting was simply saving me time and embarrassment. I had to lie to myself to make it okay because I was powerless in the situation. But in truth, I was upset because nobody knew or seemed to care that I had NFL hopes and dreams.

As a result of this, my resentment toward my mother grew. Where was she? I didn't know her anymore. My brother and I were suffering and she was nowhere to be found. Even when she was around physically, mentally she was unavailable. It was difficult to see the other kids laughing and enjoying their high school experience—playing sports, joining clubs and fitting in with the kids in our peer group—while my experience consisted of hiding and enduring. I blamed my mother for this and for the fact that I couldn't play football. By the age of 15, my dream of playing in the NFL was shattered.

However, all was not lost. David stayed on the wrestling team, and our friendship grew. We were now like brothers. This was important, because apart from the Childress family, I had little support at any of my wrestling matches. Once, Aunt Kate and Uncle Lawrence brought their family to one of my tournaments at Ruskin High School in Kansas City. But most of the time, I felt alone. Despite this, my sophomore wrestling season was a success and I was gaining confidence in my ability fight and drive myself to victory—no matter the arena.

Hand in the Register

By the summer after my sophomore year we were forced to give up our little attic apartment at 3538 Garfield and move in with my mother's boyfriend—a man my brother and I had barely met. His house was no better. It was a small-decayed shack that reeked of mildew because of a leaky roof and had no running hot water. The insecurity of living in another dump was only topped by the fact that it wasn't ours. Once again, we were living in someone else's space and at the mercy of their acceptance of us. One false move and we could be on the streets again.

My only saving grace that summer was that I was going back to work for my uncle, and I didn't have to spend much time at home. I had done every job there was to do in my uncle's warehouse. I had sweated for four long summers in the exhausting Kansas City heat and humidity, and in the summer of 1987, after much lobbying, he agreed to allow me to work in his retail stores.

This was huge for me. I was no longer going to have to bear the heat and grime of warehouse work. Now I would get to work in the clean, air-conditioned environment of one of his stores. This meant I would have energy left over at the end of the day.

It was also the summer I turned sixteen, which meant that like most 16-year olds, I had two things on my mind: getting my driver's license and saving to buy a car. Buying a car was probably not realistic with our financial struggles. But I was enchanted by the idea. Many of the kids that I went to school with got cars for their sixteenth birthdays or had unlimited access to their parents cars. Although my family wasn't like the families I went to school with, I couldn't help trying to keep up with them. My self-esteem could only take so much; I wanted desperately to belong and a car would go a long way in appeasing me.

Each morning I would get ready for work and wait on Uncle Lawrence to pick me up. My mother, half asleep, would be in her long blue housecoat helping get her boyfriend off to work. She did nothing else. As far as I knew, she sat around all day watching "The Young & The Restless", smoking weed, and drinking beer while I was busting my tail. I began to lose respect for her. At 16, I felt I had a superior work ethic, and I was trying hard to make things better.

Then several weeks into the summer, she approached me and asked, "Can I borrow some money?"

My heart sank. I had known this was coming. "How much?"

"Two hundred dollars. I'll pay you back when I get my (welfare) check." I had heard this song and dance every summer since I was 11 years old. She would ask and I would never have the courage to say no. How do you deny your mother? Begrudgingly, I gave her the $200. But I knew my money was gone as soon as it left my hands.

A week later, my mother's check came in. My brother and I always looked forward to that day because the refrigerator and cupboards would get stocked with food that was supposed to last the entire month but very rarely did. That night when I got home from work, I waited with nervous anticipation for my mother to pay me my money back. She went to bed that evening with no mention of it. The week went by in the same way: me waiting nervously, my mother not even acknowledging that she had borrowed $200 from me with the promise to pay me back.

That weekend, I approached her. "Hey mom. You got your check. I was wondering when you were going to pay me my money back." With a scathing eye, she hissed, "Boy! I raised you! I put a roof over your head! I've bought you clothes, food…" she ranted on, and I simply wanted to disappear.

I retreated into my room with tears in my eyes, feeling victimized. Deep down, I knew that my mother would ask again and again to "borrow" my hard-earned money and that I would never see it again. How was I ever going to buy my car?

That summer, my desire for a car and my frustration led me to do the unthinkable: I began stealing cash from the register at my uncle's retail store. When a customer made a purchase, instead of ringing up the sale I would put the cash in my pocket. After all the things my uncle had done for me through the years, I was betraying his trust, and I felt terrible for it. But I was so physically and emotionally bankrupt at the time that my internal compass was simply not functioning correctly.

Over several weeks, I stole about $800. With $700 that I was able to save from my paychecks, I had $1,500 for a down payment on a new 1987 candy apple red Yugo GV with a manual transmission. I didn't even know how to drive a stick shift, but it didn't matter. I had my car.

Crash

Right away the car became a source of conflict between my mother and me. At 16, armed with a driver's license and a car, I couldn't be told much. But to my mother, that did not mean I could do what I wanted to do when I wanted to do it. As a matter of fact, even though I was paying for the car, she tried to control it. When I began to try to tell her what I was going to do, as opposed to asking, she would have none of it. My desire for freedom versus her need to control me caused us to argue. Over time our arguments became increasingly bitter. We were in the middle of a power struggle.

But while my mother couldn't slow me down, the events of a warm August night in 1987 could. I'd had my driver's license for just over one month and my car for less than that. My brother and I were leaving my aunt and uncle's house with the radio cranked full bore, listening to LL Cool J's "Rock the Bells". We were mesmerized by the beat and having a great time bobbing our heads. Neither of us was wearing a seat belt at the time.

As we approached the busy intersection on Bennington Avenue and Blue Parkway, I clicked the left turn signal and came to a stop. It was a busy and dangerous intersection, but we had been at that stop sign hundreds if not thousands of times as passengers. I looked left and saw no cars. I looked right and began to pull out. My plan was to pull into the center median, which I had seen my aunt, uncle, and mom do at that intersection in order to merge into traffic. If you didn't do that, you would never be able to cross the intersection because of its heavy traffic patterns.

But when I looked back to the left, to my horror I saw three sets of headlights coming at us at high speed—on a two-lane road. I stomped on the accelerator and tried to turn hard into the median. I didn't make it: the front end of my car was hit and began to spin into oncoming traffic. My body was hanging out the window at the waist.

When the car stopped spinning, I could feel glass shards and warm liquid all over my face and body. I jumped out of the car in a panic and ran around to the passenger side where I found Montez's head and face covered in blood. At impact, he had gone flying head first into the windshield. "Montez!" I shouted over and over hysterically. Knowing I had to get help, I ran into a trailer park across the road, found the pay phone there, dialed the operator, made a collect call to my mother and told her we were in a car accident.

"Where's Montez? Is he okay?" she asked frantically.

"He's bleeding mommy!"

"I'm on my way."

In a panic I raced back to the car. I couldn't even recognize my brother through the lacerations and blood. One of my aunt and uncle's neighbors, Mara Brock Akil—now a famous Hollywood writer and producer—happened to be in the area and was standing next to the car with her hands clasped together covering her mouth and nose in terror. I remembered that I had a towel in my wrestling bag, and I used it to clean the blood, glass, and oil from my brother's head and face. He was coherent, thank God.

Within minutes, an ambulance pulled up and paramedics began their triage. Shortly after, my mother came running up to the car in tears. A woman approached my mother and said, "Ma'am, I saw everything. It wasn't their fault. Those cars were racing." My mother nodded, but she was more concerned about getting her 14-year-old baby to the hospital.

At Children's Mercy Hospital, Montez required many stitches in his forehead to close the lacerations. My mother and I didn't leave his side. It hurt me to see him in so much pain. That night couldn't have ended soon enough. Two things that I took away from the experience: first, despite her problems my mother really did love us ferociously. Second, I was never without my seatbelt again. Being inches from possibly being decapitated changed my view on car safety. I knew we'd both been fortunate to survive that night.

Junior Year 1987-1988

I was sixteen as my junior year started, with a little hair on my upper lip. I was working hard and I thought I knew enough to be a man—at least in terms of being able to decide what was best for me. What 16-year-old doesn't think he or she is smarter than the adults in his or her life? However, in hindsight, one thing that's clear to me now is how little I really knew.

The only real discipline I ever learned was from wrestling. It singlehandedly was the best thing that ever happened to me. Much of the success I've experienced in life I credit to the toughness and grit I learned from the sport. Many times, when life got tough, I would want to quit but that's when the mental training from wrestling kicked in. I learned in order to live on the highest possible plane I had to be willing to go to the dark side. The dark side is a mental and spiritual vortex where I had to be willing to go battle to be the best I could be; where my desire to succeed had to transcend the pain required to rise. It's the closest you can ever come to death without actually dying.

I learned that when I thought there was nothing left of my strength or will, that I actually had reserves I'd never ever tapped. Tapping them is like having an out-of-body experience. I've had many points in my life when I was trapped and there seemed to be no way out, but I never gave up because of the training and mental toughness I acquired as a result of being a wrestler.

On the wrestling mat, I knew when my opponent was defeating me. I knew when all the visible evidence said that I was doomed and I had every reason in the world to quit. When my opponent was blocking my mouth and nose and I couldn't breathe, I could have ended the pain and embarrassment easily. I could have lay down and let myself be pinned in a way that no one else would know. But I would know that I had given up, and that was unacceptable to me. Junior year I made up my mind, you're going to have to kill me to stop me. That became my mantra for life. I would never quit. When the match was over, win, lose or draw, you were going to know you were in a fight.

Wrestling had many parallels to what I was experiencing in life. I was fighting to survive. In wrestling you to have to fight to win, and I would do anything to come out on top. My hunger to win came from the pain of my hurting soul and my desire to be seen and felt, and it led me to make tremendous, sometimes, unwise, sacrifices. When I was over the weight limit for my weight class and faced with dropping weight or sitting out the week's match, I would do anything to make weight. I didn't want to let my team down. So I would starve myself. Immediately after practice I would go to the boiler room and layer up with sweat shirts and sweat pants over the top of my sauna suit, then I would jump rope until I lost as much weight as I could. Other times, I would put on my sauna suit and run six miles after practicing for three hours. I was probably close to death from heatstroke more times than I'll ever know.

Once, I lost fifteen pounds in two weeks and learned a hard lesson. I was 127 pounds and needed to get down to 112 pounds to wrestle in the annual varsity Christmas Invitational Tournament we hosted at my school. However, the night before the tournament I was still four pounds overweight! I had starved myself for days and was completely dehydrated, but not making the weight limit was not an option.

When I got home I ran several miles. Then I put on my sauna suit and several sweatshirts and sweatpants, turned the thermostat to 80 degrees and jumped into bed. I covered up with two regular blankets and an electric blanket turned on high. Not surprisingly, I tossed and turned all night.

The next morning, I weighed in at 112 pounds on the nose. Because I was famished and dehydrated, I consumed as much food and water as I could before the tournament began. The result was completely predictable: when I stepped on to the mat that morning for my first match, I started puking up everything. I felt like dying. I was sick for hours after and all I could do was sit and watch my team compete. By the time I went home that evening, I weighed 125 pounds. I had gained 13 pounds in mere hours from consuming primarily Gatorade.

The lesson? Sometimes winning isn't about reaching a goal. Sometimes, it's about doing things the right way. I'd done them the wrong way and taken myself out of the competition. But this lesson wasn't quite driven home yet. I would have to experience one more major, almost fatal, defeat in the years to come before I would grasp it.

My junior year also saw the only time that my mother ever came to one of my matches. It was a home dual and I was wrestling a guy from Fort Osage High School. I'd beaten him about two weeks prior at a wrestling invitational, so I felt confident that I could beat him again. But this time, I wanted to annihilate him to show my mother that I was good at this sport.

The match was close until the third and final period. I was down by one point and I panicked because I didn't want to lose in front of my mother to a guy I knew I could beat. Out of desperation I tried a move called a Granby, where I would flip him onto the mat and take control of the match. Unfortunately, it didn't work because I wasn't in the proper position to execute the move. But I tried to force it anyway and I ended up on my back, bridging for the final minute of the match, refusing to be pinned. But time ran out, and I lost.

I was devastated. I had lost what might be my only chance to show my mother what I could do. In my mind, if she saw my triumph it would change things. She would love me enough to get her own fighting spirit back and we would fight the world together. But I lost.

In a childish rage, I threw my headgear, costing my team a one-point penalty for my poor sportsmanship. I stormed out of the gymnasium and went down into the locker room. There, I screamed, "I quit! I quit!" and sobbed like a brokenhearted little boy. Uncle Lawrence and my mother were the only two people in the world who I cared to impress, and I failed again. I'd internalized that a failure wasn't worth loving or sacrificing for.

A few minutes later, Coach Hauck walked into the locker room.

"You had no right to act that way and get a point deducted from the team," he said in a voice as stern as stone.

"I quit!" I wailed through my tears.

"That's fine. But you owe both teams an apology," he said as he headed back to the rest of the team.

After several minutes, I collected myself and made my way back up to the gymnasium. I apologized to both teams, my mother and to Coach Hauck, and I showed up to practice the next day. I learned another valuable lesson about keeping my composure and not quitting. But I still couldn't shake the feeling that I had failed in what would become the one and only opportunity I would get to show my mother that I was worth fighting for.

Nicole and Mom

During Christmas break that year, I met and fell in love with a girl, Nicole. We met at a teen nightclub called "Down Under". She was the first girl to ever show that she desired me. I lost my virginity to her the first night we met on the floor of a movie theater I used to clean after hours. A few days after that amazing experience, I woke up to a burning sensation as I used the restroom. By far, it was the greatest pain I had ever felt. Nicole had given me "The Clap".

In spite of this, I was enchanted with how she made me feel physically and emotionally, and being with her that night was beyond anything I'd ever experienced. I was hooked, and I would've done just about anything to experience that climatic euphoria as often as possible. As I fell deeper and deeper for Nicole (despite the fact that she cheated on me constantly), I began to throw caution to the wind. I began to sneak out of the house on school nights to see her. My grades slipped. I got two Ds in the third quarter of the school year because I was daydreaming about Nicole or sleeping in my classes. I had lost my focus.

I was growing up too fast, and I wanted what I wanted. The biggest casualty of this was my relationship with my mother. The older I got, the more I disliked the fact that she controlled me and dictated how I used my hard-earned money. I was so obsessed with being with Nicole I would do anything to be with her. Sex, like drugs, can become an addiction and make people lose their minds. I was using it to cope, and I didn't want to live by my mother's rules anymore. But in her mind, she was still the head dog and some 16-year-old kid was not going to run the show. We were locked in a power struggle and it was going to come to a head.

One day, Nicole and I were walking around the shopping mall near her grandmother's home, where she lived. We walked into a jewelry store and looked at gold chains. In the late 1980s, gold chains were a big deal, but I'd never been a big jewelry guy—that is until Nicole told me she thought I would look good wearing one. With my next paycheck I went back to that mall and spent $140 on a gold chain. But I hid it from my mother because I knew she would be furious that I had spent my money on something she would deem frivolous.

A few days later, my mother approached me and said, "Let me borrow a few dollars." We'd been down this road before. "Borrow" to her meant, "Take and never give back." I was tired of this. Plus, I had no money; I'd spent it on the gold chain.

"I don't have any money," I said, nervously.

"You just got paid," she replied in a tight tone that implied I had best give her what she asked for—now. But I was getting tired of handing my hard-earned money over to her. I was tired of feeling bullied. It was my money. I earned it. I was tired of justifying being a young man who wanted to enjoy the fruits of his hard work.

"I spent it."

"On what?"

I froze. I knew how she would react. I saw her nostrils flaring.

"I bought myself a gold chain."

My mother's eyes lit up with fury. "A gold chain? Oh, you're taking that back!"

"No, I'm not mom. I bought this with my own money," I replied. I was try-ing not to be disrespectful, but I also wanted to stand up for what I believed was right.

"You're taking it back!"

"No I'm not mom. I'm keeping it."

That did it. My mother went off on me. Shrieking and out of control, she called me selfish and reminded me of many of the things that she had done to care for me over the years. To her, I was ungrateful and disrespectful.

I hadn't intended to defy my mother. But for years, I felt she had been using me and forcing me to fend for myself. All I had ever wanted was to be like other kids—to have a parent who cared for me and didn't force me to be an adult before I was ready. I'd had enough. It was time.

I called my best friend, David, and asked him to pick me up. I went into my room and began to pack my clothes in a black garbage bag. I heard David pull up outside and honk his horn. I grabbed my bag and I walked out of the room. My mother was sitting on the sofa and she said, "Boy what are you doing?"

"I'm leaving."

She stood up. "You ain't going nowhere!" She moved to block the door.

"Mom move. I'm leaving." I didn't want to put my hands on my mother and physically move her. But I was not staying there anymore.

She said, "If you're leaving, then I'm leaving too!" And she stepped aside.

At that, Montez started to cry, saying "What about me? What about me?" I looked at him; he was terrified about the prospect of being left alone with no mother and no brother, just my mother's boyfriend.

I threw my garbage bag over my shoulder and walked out the door. David was sitting there in his car waiting for me. I got in and we drove away.

The Childresses

For a while, I lived with my Aunt Kate and Uncle Lawrence, but that didn't last long. Within a month, Aunt Kate had kicked me out. She didn't want me there. I couldn't go back to living with my mother, and that's when Cheryl and Chuck Childress, David's parents, took me in.

I moved in with them and they gave me my own room and treated me just like a son. They talked to me just like I was their own. The only difference was that I wasn't. They were warm and loving, but inside I longed to be someone's real son. Someone who had a parent or parents who stood up like parents were supposed to and gave me something to aspire to—who were my blood parents, not an aunt or an uncle, not my best friend's parents, but my own flesh and blood. It hurt not being with my own family, but I had to survive. The Childresses didn't make me feel like an outsider; they included me in everything, even their family talks. David and I continued to wrestle and I continued to flourish in the sport.

I think a lot of my success in wrestling had to do with channeling my anger and frustration. Things weren't working very well in my family life and wrestling was a way for me to pour that negative energy into something productive. It was an outlet; a way for me to learn how to fight for my own life. So I did.

Senior Year 1988-1989

Senior year is supposed to be a happy time for young men and women; adulthood beckons, leading to college, employment and freedom. Not for me. I entered my senior year filled with anxiety. Instead of looking toward the future with excitement, I was looking toward it with fear. I had no idea what my future held and it scared me. So I did what I had always done since moving to Kansas City: I faked like I knew where I was going and what I was doing.

At least I had done a decent job with my academic work. I would graduate. I had completed all the requisite classes and I would have all the credits necessary to graduate after the first semester. It was my senior year, so I wanted to have as much fun as I could, given all the unknowns that lay in front of me.

David was on track to graduate on time, too. When he signed up for a business class that allowed him to leave campus every day at 11 a.m. to work, I did the same. He would go to his job and I'd go to mine, working for my uncle. It was important to me to make as much money as I could. Even though David's parents didn't ask me to pay rent, I wanted to be as little of a burden on them as I could be. I was determined to support myself. The wounded 12-year-old boy inside would not allow me to ask them to borrow money for lunch—or anything for that matter. I felt compelled to absorb the cost of things on my own as much as I could.

But it didn't take long for me to realize that the money I was making working part-time wasn't going to be enough to have the charmed senior year I wanted. When Jostens came to school to take orders for class rings, I had to live vicariously through David as his parents shelled out $700 for his ring. Just like in every other instance where I felt left out, I lied to myself and minimized the importance of the milestone. "You don't even like to wear jewelry," I told myself. That was true. But it wasn't the point. A class ring would have been a symbol of a normal high school experience—at least in the suburban school I attended. Instead, my ring finger remained naked.

I did my best to feel good for David as he enjoyed the year of his life. But inside, I was hurt and envious. So I started drinking more. David and I began experimenting with alcohol. Neither one of us really enjoyed the taste. However, we both liked the buzz. David never became much of a drinker. I, on the other hand, began to excel at it. Once I became accustomed to the bitter taste of beer, I began to drink more and more. By senior year, I had moved on from beer and started to drink fortified wine like the legendary Mad Dog 20/20. It wasn't long before I was passing out and nursing hangovers that felt as miserable as my terrible self-esteem and sense of loneliness.

Money Over Wrestling

As my miserable, lonely year was playing out, the only thing that made me feel better about myself was having money in my pocket. Money was the great equalizer. David and I were hard workers and were not afraid to work multiple jobs in order to keep our pockets full. However, when wrestling season started in late fall, there would be no way I could leave school, catch a bus to the inner city to go to work, and then catch a bus after work from the inner city back to the suburbs in time for wrestling practice.

I had to make a difficult decision. I couldn't do everything. I didn't have the kind of support that David did. His parents were good to me, but their priority was their son and rightly so. While they let him drive their second car to and from his job, I was left to fend for myself; as usual.

In the end, money won out over wrestling. Having money was my top priority. I couldn't live with people and not be able to care for myself. My pride would not allow me to be a burden. I had to work. That meant that I had to quit wrestling. It was one of the most agonizing decisions I have ever made in my life. My dream of qualifying for the Missouri state wrestling tournament was gone, just like my NFL dreams. It's one of my deepest regrets.

After I walked away from wrestling, I was agitated. I tried to keep a cheery demeanor, but inside I was hurt and angry. I stopped caring about life. Wrestling had given me something to work on, to channel my anger and resentment over my poverty and my mother's actions. Once it was taken away from me, I checked out. I started drinking more and having as much sex as I could.

This was also the first time I thought seriously about selling drugs. Crack cocaine had become extremely popular. The guys who were selling drugs had money, cars and women. All three would have definitely helped me forget my problems.

I'd grown tired of feeling like everyone's burden and wanted to take care of myself. I thought long and hard about dealing. Fortunately, I never had the courage to risk it. I knew that if I did and my uncle found out, he would kick my butt. His approval was one of the few bright spots in my life at the time and I didn't want to risk losing his respect. I knew he wouldn't condone a drug-dealing nephew for a New York minute. He would cut me off and slam the door behind me.

My senior year was flying by, yet I had no direction. I spent all my time hurt and angry. I was even having thoughts of suicide. I felt like no one would miss me, and that I didn't have much to live for. I was terrified of the future. I knew the time was coming when people would stop seeing me as the poor kid who needed help and instead as a young man who needed to get his life together.

But I was scared. I didn't know what to do or where to go. I tried to stay as close to David and his parents as I could. However, they weren't my parents and while they did their best, they didn't have the resources to give me everything I needed.

For example, one of the most memorable events of a student's high school experience is prom. Prom was out of the question for me. I didn't have a tux. I didn't have a car. So as usual, I watched David and others do what I was aching to do, and acted as if it didn't matter.

Graduation

Most critical of all, I had no idea where I was going after graduation. I couldn't live with the Childress family forever. David was going off to college, and I certainly wasn't going to stay behind in his home when he left! So, when he began to apply for colleges and universities, I applied with him.

I was open to anyplace. I just wanted to get away from Kansas City, Misery. I had no clue how I was going to go to college. I didn't have two nickels to rub together. I just went along for the ride. It was a pastime, a diversion, dreaming that I would be able to pay for college.

Then, both David and I got accepted into the University of Wyoming in Laramie. I don't know how we chose to apply to Wyoming, the least populous and least racially diverse state in the Lower 48, but we did. David's parents scheduled a campus visit for both of us, and in April 1991 we flew into Laramie, Wyoming.

The entire experience was amazing. I was 17 and it was the first time I had ever been on an airplane. We spent four days living in the dorms on the campus getting a real college experience. During our visit, we met a couple of really cool guys and ended up partying with them. I met a girl named Ali, a sweet and kindhearted young lady. I had never had so much fun in my life. Wyoming started looking really good to me. If that was what college life was all about, there was no way in the world I was going to miss out. But first I had to finish high school.

Graduation day finally arrived, and I had heard through the grapevine that my mother, who I hadn't spoken to since moving in with the Childress's a year and a half earlier, was going to attend the ceremony. The afternoon of the ceremony, David and I picked up two girls and a cooler full of beer and wine coolers and went to a quiet, secluded area of Swope Park and got drunk.

We drank until the last possible minute, leaving us just enough time to make it back to David's house and get ready for the ceremony. I was nervous because I hadn't seen my mother in forever. I was dreading the awkwardness of our reunion. The confrontation on the day I moved out kept replaying in my mind. It wasn't that I didn't love my mother; I disliked her behavior and what she had put my brother and I through. But like it or not, I was going to have to face her.

As our evening graduation ceremony approached, the adrenaline rush overwhelmed the alcohol buzz. Graduation. I could hardly believe it. Less than one year earlier, I had been seriously contemplating dropping out of school.

Life had simply become too hard. Education wasn't what I needed. What I needed was money. Money was my problem. But I'd learned through the years of working for my uncle that hard work would remedy that problem. Somehow, my learned work ethic and perseverance had gotten me to the finish line.

Once dressed, we loaded into the Childress family van and drove to the auditorium. I knew my mother would be there along with my brother, Aunt Kate, Uncle Lawrence and my younger cousins. I didn't get the opportunity to see them before the ceremony started because David and I were whisked off to a separate area where all the graduates sat until we walked on the stage to receive our diplomas.

By the time the graduation ceremony began that evening, I had sobered up, but I was still under the influence. Sitting in the auditorium chair awaiting the processional, I began to get emotional. The magnitude of the occasion finally hit me. For most people, graduating from high school is an automatic, an expectation. I wished that all I had to contend with were books, teachers, homework and hormones. Instead, I'd confronted poverty, near-homelessness, a narrow escape car accident, violence and an addicted mother. That I'd come through to this point utterly overwhelmed me.

As tears of joy and pain fell down my face, the ceremony processional began. As we slowly made our way onto the stage, each graduate sought out the loving faces of friends and family members who had come to celebrate their achievement. I scoured the audience to see my family. I couldn't see nor hear them. There was so much excitement. People were screaming, "I love you!" and whistling. Then, as I took the stage to receive my diploma, I heard clapping and screams from both my family and the Childress family. I walked off that stage proud, with that piece of paper in my hand.

After the ceremony, we met up with our family and friends. The first person I saw was Montez. As I began to approach him for a hug, I saw my mother. It had been too long since I had last seen or talked to her; the tension between us was an elephant in the room. I hugged my brother and my mother, my aunt, my uncle, and the whole Childress family.

As congratulatory hugs and well wishes were being handed out all over the place, David and I were the centers of attention. A decision was made: the celebration was going to move to the Childress home. My mother was my mother.

Yet the Childress family had taken me in and treated me more like a son than my mother had the past year and a half.

Despite the awkwardness, we began our journey back to the Childress home. I rode with the Childresses. I felt like I had been forced to choose sides and chosen wrong. After everyone arrived and was making their way inside the house, my mother tapped my shoulder, "Can I talk to you?" She asked

"Okay."

It was awkward. I didn't want to discuss why I left home. I didn't want to make my mother feel worse than she probably already felt watching me celebrate my graduation with another family. I didn't want her to think I didn't love her. I didn't want to fight. We turned around and walked back out to the driveway of the Childress home.

"I'm sorry," my mother said as she began to cry.

The sight of her tears and pain caused me to begin crying, too. No more words were needed. We hugged. I loved my mother. No one could ever replace her. I badly wanted her to be there for Montez and me. But she couldn't. She didn't know how to be a mother any longer. She was suffering. We weren't children anymore, and instead of telling us what to do, her role was to listen to us and teach us how to be adults. My mother was incapable of either one. She was sick from the pain of her life, lost in depression and addicted to drugs and alcohol. We hugged for several minutes, a silent acknowledgement of this reality.

"I love you," she said, her arms wrapped tightly around me.

"I love you too, Mom." Tears rolling down my face.

In our heart of hearts we both knew that this was goodbye. I had come of age. Things were never going to be the same. That cold winter night, when I left home at the age of sixteen, was the end of the road for us. I was less than two months from turning eighteen and I was never coming home again. So I thought. We had been through so much. Too much damage had been done. Our hug was about forgiveness. I forgave my mother for not being there for my brother and me, and I think she forgave me for leaving.

We dried our eyes and walked back into the Childress home. I could sense that everyone was waiting to hear that we had reconciled and that I would be returning home. That would not be the case. When the celebration ended, my mother returned to her life with my brother by her side.

CHAPTER 7

WHY-OMING?

It was August 1989. I had turned 18 one month earlier. Excitement was building for David and me as we anticipated becoming college students. I wasn't sure how I'd found a way to afford college, but I had applied for and was approved for financial aid and before long I'd be on my way.

When the day came for us to leave for Laramie, my excitement was tempered with disappointment. After all, it was most an important event in my life and my mother was not around to be a part of it. She seemed to exist in her own bubble. However, even this didn't keep me from being excited about this new chapter.

Finally, aunt Kate, her youngest son, Larry, Cheryl Childress and her daughter, Neko, and David and I drove north on I-29 and connected to I-80 west towards Wyoming. It felt like the pain of my past was disappearing in the rearview mirror. College is where kids go who are destined for the good life. It's a rite of passage. Without college, I would be stuck in the same hopelessness that had hovered over the first 18 years of my life like a dark cloud. To be sure, I still had challenges. I had grown up "street" and moving to a rural college campus in the mountains 700 miles away from home would test my emotional maturity. But I was looking forward to it.

Eventually, we pulled into Laramie. It was a city, but with a population of around 30,000 it was much smaller than Kansas City. Still, I started to get excited. The great time that David and I had during our official visit back in April was still fresh in my mind. I hoped to hook up with the guys we met and was looking forward to reconnecting with that girl, Ali. All I could think about was how much fun it was going to be.

As our blue van approached White Hall, the twelve-story dormitory that would be our residence, I was bubbling with anticipation. I had a sense of freedom that I had never had before. For the first time in my life, I would have my own place and no one could kick me out. It was mine. I didn't have to put on a show for anyone. I didn't have to be on my best behavior. In my mind, the roof I had over my head was not based on me fulfilling a set of conditions.

That was what I believed. However, I was about to learn that freedom is a privilege that, if not respected, can be taken away.

Ali

The campus was active with students and their families helping them move into their dorm rooms. It reminded me of the fact that, on some level, I was going through this experience by myself. I would have loved nothing more than to have the kind of family that could be there to celebrate with me. However, I wouldn't let my circumstances steal my joy.

As we unloaded the van and set up our new living quarters, I thought about all the things I needed to accomplish that day, from buying stuff for our dorm room to going to the financial aid office to ensure that my loans had come in. I had worked hard the entire summer to be able to pay for everything. But when I got to the financial aid office that day, I was informed my loans hadn't been funded yet. As a result, I was forced to take out a short-term bridge loan from the university until my loans were funded. It was also brought to my attention that I was going to be short a few thousand dollars for the year. I had no idea how I was going to make ends meet. I, naively, believed that it would just work out.

The next day, Aunt Kate, Cheryl, Neko and Larry made the long ten-hour trek back to Kansas City. When the van pulled away, it was official. I was a college student. My fear was beginning to dissipate, but it would be a long time before I completely let my guard down. I was still a kid with, essentially, no home and no family. I wasn't only trying to figure out how to be a college student; I was going to have to figure out how to live in the world as a so-called young adult.

After settling in, the first thing I wanted to do was to see Ali, the girl I had met in April. She was a short, brown-haired, brown-eyed white girl with a pretty smile. She'd been born and raised in Laramie and attended the local high school, where she was entering her senior year. She had an older brother and sister, who were both adopted before her birth because her parents didn't believe they could conceive children of their own. Her mother and father had been divorced for years and she had chosen to live with her father. He was a University of Wyoming alum and a well-respected businessman in Laramie.

Ali's mother was an alcoholic who remarried and lived in Idaho. Sadly, the only time Ali would really ever hear from her mother was when she'd been drinking. She would call Ali in a drunken stupor and lay a guilt trip on her for not calling and never visiting. Our grief over our lost mothers was something we bonded over.

Ali's dad was a great provider, but he was tough and had high expectations for his children. Ali revered her father, who had taken on the responsibility of raising her and her siblings. As a result, she was fearful of doing anything that would disappoint or bring shame on him—including dating outside of her race. She'd told me right away that her father probably wouldn't approve of us dating. During our relationship, she would lie more than once to avoid the possibility of disappointing or angering him.

After our first meeting back in April, she and I had stayed in touch and got to know each other better by regularly writing letters and making long distance phone calls, and I couldn't wait to spend time with her. It was just one more reason to be excited about college.

Fish Out of Water

My first full day as a college student was on the Friday before classes began. There was a lot of buzz about the parties that were going on and I was planning to take them all in. I had waited my whole life to be an irresponsible kid and just have fun. Something inside me knew this was my time, and I was determined to be indoctrinated into the full college experience—minus the books and studying, of course.

David and I had fake IDs made for us in Kansas City. Although they looked fake too, we never had a problem using them. Bars and clubs in Laramie seemed to invite underage drinking. Laramie didn't see many African-Americans, and the ones they did see were mostly scholarship athletes that played on the university's sports teams. If you were an athlete in a small town like Laramie, you got preferential treatment and immediate respect. Neither David nor I came to town on an athletic scholarship, but I never skipped an opportunity to use my ethnicity to my advantage. Whether it was buying alcohol at the local liquor store, gaining access to a local bar or gaining favor with some of the college girls looking to increase their popularity by befriending an athlete, I played the role.

David and I quickly met many of the students on the floor of our dormitory, most of whom were new to the university like us. As it turned out, the party would never leave our dorm that night. Within 36 hours of arriving in Laramie, I had been cordially introduced to the beer bong.

The first beer went down with ease. The next dozen or so were nothing. That was the night I was also introduced to two other new concepts: blacking out and throwing up. I would master both during my tenure at the University of Wyoming, earning a PhD in them. David would nurse me back to sobriety, a pattern that would repeat itself over and again.

I began drinking at 16, but I had never drunk as much as I did that night. Drinking represented a new and exciting experience for me, an escape from my insecurities. But I also wanted to impress my new friends. College was supposed to enable me to forget my past and build my future, and if getting smashed and blacking out was escaping my past and building my future, then mission accomplished!

My first day of classes came the following Monday morning. I rose early, excited. I felt like pinching myself. I'm not sure how I had gotten here, but I had. I didn't know what to expect, so I reverted to my default response: just do what everybody else is doing. I put my backpack on and walked to my first class, English 101.

It was a small classroom with about 30 students. This gave me a sense of comfort because it was just like high school. No big deal. "Write a couple of papers and get an easy A," I thought as I took my seat. The professor introduced herself and passed out the syllabus. That's when I realized that college was going to be a little more work than I expected. Still, I thought, "No big deal." If I hadn't learned any other thing in life to this point, I had learned how to work hard.

My next class was Macroeconomics, and it was a stark contrast to my 30-student English class. I had heard about these mega-lecture courses, but until I saw one with my own eyes I couldn't quite wrap my mind around the idea. When I entered the lecture hall there were between 200 and 300 seats, most of them occupied. I wondered how one professor could teach so many students and be responsible for their learning? I found out quickly that in the mega-lecture classes, the professor isn't necessarily concerned about whether you understand the material or concepts. That's your responsibility. If you don't understand a concept, you best head to the graduate teaching assistant's office, the professor's office, or someone in the class who knows what the heck is going on. Otherwise, you're in for a rough ride. On the outside, I was a cool as the other side of the pillow. On the inside, I was nervous and fretting, wondering if I was going to be able to pass the class.

One thing that led me to believe I was not going to be babysat was the fact that there was no roll call. The professor didn't know if I was in class or not. Nor did he care. I had been accepted into the university, the assumption was that I was adult enough to make it to lecture hall without my hand being held. My actions were to challenge that assumption.

I only had two classes that first day, but I was overwhelmed. In many ways, I felt that I had no business being there. I felt like I was pretending to be a college student and just like Cinderella, the midnight hour would chime and I would turn back into a pumpkin—an impoverished pumpkin with an addicted mother.

Ladies' Man

Getting acclimated to the rigorous academic lifestyle was a huge challenge. Socially, however, I was a Rhodes scholar. With only 24 hours in the day, I found myself operating on the "just-in-time" system of preparation. When exams came, I would cram for them the night before.

I also found myself dealing with my identity as a black male and the misconception that all black men are great athletes, great dancers, and smooth talkers. Attending a university whose student body was more than 95 percent white, in a state with the same racial profile, made me feel like I had too much to live up to. I wasn't attending Wyoming on an athletic scholarship like the majority of African-Americans on campus, nor did I think I was a great dancer. Just like in high school, I could only see myself through what I lacked. In order to fit in, I felt like I had to play into the stereotype.

In my mind, that meant creating an identity for myself through my success with the ladies. In order to build my "cool factor" and feel like a stud around the other guys (black and white), I started to flirt with girls—lots of them. While this didn't really suit my personality it seemed to calm my insecurities, as well as appeasing my raging 18-year-old hormones.

It wasn't long before this got me into hot water. My next-door neighbor in the dorms was Chris Michaels. Chris was from a small town in Wyoming and must have come from a pretty affluent family because he drove a brand new Ford Probe. Chris was a pretty cool guy, but I could tell that he hadn't spent much time around people of other races. He seemed to be awkward when it came to understanding diversity. I never held that against him though.

Chris had several friends from his hometown who were attending UW. One was Kristi. Kristi was a petite brunette with pretty brown eyes and beautiful short hair. I happened to spot her visiting Chris's room one day and thought she was cute. When she left, I asked him about her. She was dating some guy in the military but they had an on again off again relationship. I asked him to introduce me to her next time she stopped by his room to say hello. But Chris didn't wait until next time she came over. He called her and told her what I had said. One thing led to the next, and we were introduced.

Over the next couple of weeks, we got to know each other, while at the same time I was dating Ali—supposedly exclusively. I knew I was violating Ali's trust, but I allowed my hormones to get the best of me and before long I was dating two girls at the same time. It was easy because Ali was a high school senior and wasn't allowed out late on weekdays. After Ali and I were done hanging out and she went home for the night, I would go hang out with Kristi. This went on for several weeks…until one evening the you-know-what hit the fan.

I played intramural sports with some of my buddies from the dorms. It was softball season and we had put a team together to compete amongst the other teams in the residence halls. Every Thursday evening we had a game. Typically, Ali would come out and watch the games and support my team, but for this one game, she was home sick with the flu. So I invited Kristi to attend.

The game went smoothly. As we changed sides between innings I would wave at Kristi and smile. This went on until the seventh inning. I was playing left field when I saw Ali's car pull up to the field. She got out and walked up to the set of four-row aluminum bleachers behind home plate. Worse yet, Ali sat right down next to Kristi and her friend! It didn't take long before I noticed them talking and Ali pointing her finger in my direction. I could only imagine what the they were saying:

Kristi: "Hi. Who are you here to watch?"

Ali: "I came to watch my boyfriend Frank. There he is out in left field."
Kristi: "He's your boyfriend? That's funny! I've been dating him for the past 3-4 weeks."

I knew I was in trouble. I could tell by their body language that they were getting to know each other. When the game was over, instead of running from the outfield to the dugout to celebrate with the rest of my team, I jumped the fence in the outfield and ran back to my room. I sat on the bed with my head in my hands, waiting.

Not long after, there was knock on the door. It was Ali, tears rolling down her cheeks. She had come to get answers. But I had nothing that would explain my childish, immature and selfish behavior. All I could do was apologize and tell her how sorry I was for hurting her. She listened, then turned and walked away.

I sat in my room trying to understand how I could have lost someone who loved me and was so special. Then my thoughts turned to Kristi. I knew I was going to have to face her, too. Instead of waiting for the other shoe to drop, I called her dorm room and asked if she would speak with me. She agreed. I apologized to her and told her that I had spoken to Ali and that we had broken up. After a long discussion, I ended up spending the night with her.

The problem was that I didn't love Kristi. We had only known each other a short time before we became physically involved. My heart was with Ali. I was in love with her. But my dysfunction was more powerful than my heart. I wanted to be liked and accepted. My buddies hailed me as The Man for having two girls at the same time. My need for acceptance was stronger than my love for Ali. I found myself with someone but all alone at the same time.

Disaster

The fall semester continued and while I missed Ali tremendously, Kristi and I continued to see each other. However, I would spend the majority of my time drinking, hanging out with my buddies in the dorms and partying at the local nightclubs. Kristi wasn't much of a partier, so the majority of our relationship took place after hours. She wanted more of my time and I wanted less of hers until eventually, the relationship ended.

Still, being single in a small college town had its benefits. Now there was nothing to keep me from partying as hard as I wanted. My drinking became heavier. Any money I had went to purchase alcohol. Late nights turned into late mornings. Hangovers were my constant companions. The only time I went to class was to take exams.

Meanwhile, David and I were hardly speaking. He had a girlfriend who was an upperclassman and lived in an off campus apartment. He was getting tired of my drunkenness and total disregard for my education, so he distanced himself from me. When he would come by the dorm room to pick up some of his things, there was more tension than connection. Though I couldn't see it, my life was fraying around the edges.

Then, one evening in the fall of 1989 the phone in the dorm room rang.

"Hello."

"Hi," the voice on the other side said, softly. It was Kristi. She had been having trouble letting go of our relationship and I was getting tired of her calls and her publicly stalking me.

"Hi Kristi," I responded in an annoyed tone.

"Can I talk to you?"

"What is it?"

"Can I come over? I need to speak with you in person."

"I don't think that's a good idea."

"It's important," she said in a way that sounded as if she was crying.

"Are you all right?" I asked.

"No. I need to talk to you."

"All right. I'm here. Come over," I said.

Kristi lived in McIntyre Hall, one of the residence halls adjacent to my building. After a few minutes, there was a knock on the door. I opened it and

Kristi walked in.

"What's up?" I said tersely. "What's so important that we needed to see each other right now?" She sat there for a second and said nothing. I could tell she was about to cry.

"I…I…I…," she stuttered, tears rolling down her face.

What in the world have I gotten myself into? She's psycho! I thought.

"I…I…I'm pregnant," she said.

The world tilted.

"What? How could this happen?" I asked. I was dumbfounded.

This is not possible.

"Remember the two times we didn't use protection?" she said.

"Yeah! But, there's no way you could've gotten pregnant!" I protested.

"Well, I did!" she shouted.

This couldn't be happening to me. From what I had seen through some of my buddies' experiences, the best thing to do was to deny it or blame it on somebody else, because 99 percent of the time, it was the girl's attempt to get you back. So I played along.

"What are you gonna do?" I asked.

"Have an abortion," she said. "But I need $300."

"I don't have $300."

"Neither do I. Can't you borrow it from someone?" she asked.

"Let me see what I can do," I said. I just wanted to end the conversation. I didn't believe her. I thought she was trying to play me. She told me she needed the money within a week because she wanted to take care of it as quickly as possible. I agreed and showed her out. From that point forward I did everything I could to avoid her. I believed if I called her bluff, she would admit she'd been lying or the problem would just go away.

Over the next two weeks, she contacted me several times a day about the $300. I ignored her.

Then, before Thanksgiving break one of my friends came to my dorm room. He knew the situation I was in with Kristi.

"Yo dog!" he said.

"Wassup?"

"I just saw Kristi at Washakie and she was walking slow and funny, like she was in pain," he said with a serious look.

"For real?"

"Yeah man! I think she had an abortion."

I simply didn't want to accept it. I felt like he was pulling my leg and trying to get a rise out of me. I wasn't buying it. Then a couple of days later, I bumped into one of Kristi's friends from her hometown. She gave me a cold look.

"Was Kristi really pregnant?" I asked. "Did she have an abortion?"

"Yes, she was. And, yes, she did. She's dropping out of school at the end of the semester. She's going back to Casper."

I felt like a creep. But there was nothing I could do. I didn't have $300. And while I was disgusted with myself and sickened by how I treated Kristi, I was also relieved I didn't have a child on the way. I couldn't even take care of myself; there was no way I would have been able to take care of a baby!

Bleak Winter

The episode with Kristi only fueled my desire to drink. I started to display full-blown alcoholic tendencies. I was losing myself. I had no self-control and my drinking would continue most nights until I vomited. Other nights, I would black out before I vomited and not remember anything that I'd said or done.

Eventually, my behavior cost me my best friend, David. He informed me that he would not be coming back to the University of Wyoming for the second semester of his freshman year. This was devastating. For four years, he and I had been inseparable. We were like Siamese twins. We finished each other's sentences! What had I done?

The fact that he'd made the decision and gone through the process of finding a transfer school hurt even more because I hadn't been part of the process. For years, I'd told myself that I was part of the Childress family. Now, it was clear that was over as well. David and I weren't brothers. I got the message. I was out.

When David's dad picked us up in Laramie to drive back to Kansas City to begin the winter break, no one told me that I was no longer welcome at the Childress home, but no one had to. I felt like I had been disqualified from the family. The hurt and neglected little boy inside felt like I had worn out my welcome. The thick, uncomfortable silence during the drive made me believe it was best for me to go back to the dilapidated drug house at 2615 Bales, where my brother and mother lived with her boyfriend, Vincent.

Not much had changed at that house, except the fact that there was more drug activity than when I had left. But I had come full circle, and my mother welcomed me back with no qualms. David and I would never regain our former closeness.

Winter brought a stiff coldness and a stark reality: I was really on my own. There was not one adult who cared for me in all the ways I needed. There was no one I could go to and share what I was experiencing. There was no one who seemed to care. My one confidante had been David, and after my drunken behavior I felt that he and his parents more tolerated than embraced me.

At the same time, my drinking was getting worse and I felt less in control of my circumstances than ever. The tipping point in my relationship with the Childress family came one evening after I attended a Christmas party at David's mother's workplace. She was a human resources manager for a popular international hotel chain, and the party had plenty of food, music and alcohol. I was downing one free drink after another and got completely loaded. David was driving and took a carload of our friends back to his house afterwards. We made our way to the basement, where we normally congregated.

Once we arrived, David tried to hide me from his parents. They were upstairs and generally let us have our privacy. However, he knew they were fed up with my drinking and was afraid they would come down to check on us.

As I rested in an armchair, a sick feeling came over me.

"I don't feel well," I told David.

David ran to grab the garbage can out of the laundry room. He told me if I had to puke that the garbage can was right there. I sat there with my eyes closed and my head spinning, feeling as if I was riding a roller coaster. Before long, someone came down the basement stairs, making everyone in the room scramble to make it look like things were normal. It was David's mother, coming to check on us. When she walked in, she found me drunk, sitting in the La-Z-Boy armchair. She was not happy.

My stomach began to boil and I turned to vomit in the garbage can that David had put beside me. However, in his panic to hide my drunkenness from his mother, he had grabbed the garbage can and stuck it back in the laundry room. The noxious stew of beer, wine, Swedish meatballs and veggies that I had consumed that evening erupted out of my mouth and all over the floor. Everyone stood there, shocked.

For several minutes I sat there, feeling awful. Then David's mother, furious, grabbed me and pulled me to a standing position. "You want a drink, huh?" she shouted. She grabbed a shot glass and a bottle of vodka, poured a shot and lifted it to my mouth, forcing me to drink it. Gagging, I spit it out and fell to the ground. She bent over, poured another shot and forced it to my lips. Again, I spit it out. She did this several times. Cursing at her, I attempted to stand up but fell down again.

"Oh! You bad now?"

The vodka, it turned out, was only water. She was trying to teach me a lesson. The next morning, I apologized to her and her husband for my behavior. The episode was over…but nothing else felt right. I didn't have anyone to turn to who was capable of helping me through this dark time. Drinking had become my answer, just like it had for my mother.

The Prison of My Mind

Winter break was weird. Everything felt out of sorts. My friendship with David and relationship with his parents had crumbled. There were unresolved issues with my mother. My drinking had become reckless. I was flunking out of college. I had lost all drive and motivation. My life was spiraling out of control. I knew I could either fight to make it better, or continue to hide from reality behind my hedonistic cravings. I chose the latter. Every action I took moved me closer to surrendering to the demons of my childhood.

Returning to live with my mother was like admitting that my dreams were hopeless. Dreams weren't for people in poverty. I felt like a slave who'd had visions of a better life. However, after spending several years in quasi-freedom, I realized that I never really escaped. The prison was in my mind.

One of the last days of my winter break, the phone rang. I didn't think much of it because no one would be looking for me at my mother's boyfriend's house. I could hear my mother speaking as if she was confused, trying to make sense of who the caller was. I knew it couldn't be good. Then came the last thing my mother said before she hung up the phone: "Well, honey, that's good because Frank don't need no kids!"

Kristi. Somehow, she had gotten my mother's phone number and told my mother I had gotten her pregnant and promised to give her $300.

My mother approached the bedroom. The door slammed open.

"Frank!" my mother shouted. "Who's Kristi?" She already knew who Kristi was. She wanted an explanation.

I just stared, fearful of my mother's words. I knew that if she—a woman who could barely care for herself, much less me—turned me away, I would have nothing.

"She's a girl at college who claims I got her pregnant," I said meekly.

At that, she turned and walked away. She didn't say another word about it. I never heard from Kristi after that. I knew I would never put myself in that position again.

King Park

The time had come to head back to school. David had transferred to Colorado State, and now I was really on my own. My mom was back in the picture, but she had her own demons. She and her boyfriend were peddling weed and small amounts of crack out of the family house. He had always smoked and sold weed, but he'd graduated to crack. Because of its highly addictive nature, once they began dealing crack the regular flow of weed buyers became a constant surge of addicts. They were also violating one of the number one street commandments: "Don't get high on your own supply." Our home had become a full-fledged dope house.

I felt bad to be leaving Montez all over again. I loved him and wanted the best for him. I knew he loved me and would do anything for me. He was a victim and had no way of escaping. But as I saw it, life was doing its best to choke me too. My only option was to hide within the confines of the educational infrastructure. But with no money, I didn't know how long that plan was going to last. I was just glad to be getting out of Kansas City.

With the Childress family no longer in the picture, my mom was forced to drive me back to college. This meant a lot to me. I wanted to show her that her oldest baby had dreams. But before we departed, she and Uncle Lawrence wanted to have a talk with me. They had gotten my grade report for the fall semester and it was hideous: one C, two D's and an F. The look on Uncle Lawrence's face felt worse than my grades. I had disappointed the only man I ever looked up to. I had put in absolutely no effort, and I was surprised my grades were that good. I promised them both I would do better.

My mother and I loaded into a rented car and we started our journey. She intended to stop in Des Moines to see if one of my cousins wanted to ride with us. I was excited to see my cousins. I missed growing up with them. Even though we would fight often, when someone had a problem with one of the cousins they had to deal with all of us. People knew there was hell to pay if you messed with the Morris kids.

I was excited about returning as a student at a Division One university. None of my older cousins had ever been to a Division One school. The ones who had gone to college went to small community colleges or Division Two or Three schools. Most didn't make it past their first year. I was going to be different. I just knew it.

Arriving in Des Moines, I wanted to find my cousin Aaron. We had always been close. He had recently come back after being discharged from the Army, and it had been a couple of years since I had seen him. We drove straight to see my Aunt Michelle, my mom's oldest sister. Aaron was Michelle's youngest son. As soon as I walked in the door I saw him. We hugged and exchanged greetings, and then the laughing and joke cracking began. We had a lot of history and we started down memory lane, reminiscing over all the adventures that we'd had living next door to each other.

Finally, I asked, "Where's Jamal?" Jamal was my oldest cousin and Aaron's older brother.

"He's up at the park," Aaron responded.

"Well, let's go over there."

Aaron and I jumped up and walked across the street. It was pitch black in the park, but Aaron knew that park like the back of his hands. We walked over to an area that was a notorious gang hangout. There I saw my oldest cousin Jamal with some of his Crip homies. They were sitting there smoking weed and drinking 40-ounce bottles of beer. These weren't the type of cats I normally hung around, but I felt safe because Jamal was there. Jamal was six-foot-

Me (on the left, ~age 5),
my mother and younger
brother in or about 1976.

Me hugging my mother goodbye the
day I moved to California (March 1991).

Me (on the right) posing with my best
friend David before prom (May 1989).

USC graduation day. I DID IT!!! (May 1999).

Me crying in my mother's arms after the USC
graduation ceremony (May 1999).

Me! The USC Leventhal School of Accounting student
commencement speaker (May 1999).

Me, the student speaker, leading the graduation processional (May 1999).

Me (on the right) working at Western Lifts in San Diego, CA (~1993).

Me (middle-on one knee) with my two oldest cousins (~1990).

My Uncle Lawrence. The man I aspired to be.

two and a feather short of 300 pounds. He got mad respect on the streets because of his gang affiliation. Nobody messed with Jamal.

As soon as we saw Jamal, he gave me some dap (a street term for handshake) and a hug.

"Man, when did you guys get into town?" he asked.

"Not too long ago."

"Where's your mom?"

"At Aunt Michelle's."

We talked for a while, and then his attention turned back to the business at hand in the park. King Park had become a well-known hangout for gangs and small-time drug dealers. It was also known to have a shooting every once in awhile. When crack hit the scene, it had changed from the nice community park where I had played basketball, freeze tag and hide and seek as a kid to a cesspool of criminal activity.

It didn't take long for things to get street. An African-American woman in her mid-thirties wearing shabby clothes walked up and began to beg for rock cocaine. The sight sickened me. But what sickened me even more was the way my cousin Jamal treated this woman, who was obviously an addict. The vile words he said to her made me sick to my stomach. It was despicable.

All I wanted to do was get out of there. How could someone treat another human being that badly? Even worse, how could someone allow themselves to be treated worse than you would treat an animal? I decided that day that I would never return to Des Moines again. Iowa, in my view, was no longer, "A Place to Grow"—like the slogan on the sign welcoming visitors to the state asserted.

After leaving the park we went back to Aunt Michelle's house. Jamal came along, and we sat in my aunt's living room talking. But I couldn't wait to leave. I had seen all that I wanted of Des Moines. I was a college student. I didn't want to be anywhere around drug-dealing or drug dealers. Drugs were the cause of many of the problems in my life and as far as I was concerned we couldn't get out of there soon enough.

During the conversation, Jamal kept boasting about how he was "the man," which was no surprise. This was commonplace in my family. We, boys, were always trying to one-up each other. But I had lost respect for Jamal after what I saw in the park. He kept on about all the money he was making selling drugs, and I wasn't impressed...until he reached into his pocket and pulled out a wad of cash the size of a baseball. I had never seen that much cash in my life. Suddenly, I was impressed. All I could think was that if I had that money, all my problems would be solved. Oh, how I ached for that money.

Back At School

It was getting late, and my mother decided it was time for us to get back on the road. Aaron had agreed to ride with us and help my mother drive back. After ten hours on the road and plenty of beer consumed on the journey, we made it. Aaron and my mom slept in my dorm room that night.

I was excited about the possibility of showing my mother and cousin around the campus the following day. But as was typical with my mom, as soon as she woke the next morning, she got back on the road home. The reality hit me: she didn't care what the campus looked like. She didn't care what it meant to me, or what it felt like to be in college. She took no interest in my journey. In fact, it felt like she resented the fact I was there and wanted no part of it.

There I sat, in an empty dorm room by myself. Even David's personal effects, which had always littered the room, were gone. I had always had Montez or David to depend on. Now it was just me. As the spring semester began, I knew if I didn't get better grades I could get kicked out of school. I was already on academic probation. But instead, I continued to look for answers in alcohol and sex.

Ali had been the only person who I felt understood me at that point, but I had mistreated her. I knew I had to get her back. Early into the spring semester I went to TD's, where she was hanging out with her friends. They despised me because of what I had done to her. As far as they were concerned, I should have been castrated with a rusty knife. I couldn't blame them, but I had to try to get Ali to forgive me.

I walked up to her and asked how she was doing. Although she was cool in her response, she didn't ignore my attempt to patch up my mistakes. After a few minutes, she warmed up to me. I could tell she didn't hate me, but she was far from being in love with me. In the end, I told her to have a great evening and departed.

A couple of days later, I found the courage to call her house. When she answered the phone, she sounded surprised to hear my voice on the other end. Our conversation lasted for a couple of hours, which was a good sign. But I didn't ask her about getting back together. I wanted her to know I was serious about being with her and wasn't playing games.

Ultimately we ended up getting back together. This time we were inseparable. If I wasn't with her, I was with my buddies in the dorms. One thing that was clear to me was that I wasn't going to jeopardize our relationship again because of my immaturity and insecurities.

Fear of Failure

When classes began that semester, Wyoming's cold hit. Subzero temperatures with several feet of snow on the ground killed the little bit of motivation I had to get to class. The snow and cold became my excuse to not get out of bed. In reality, I was too tired and hung over. Getting up early in the morning was impossible. Sleeping off the previous night's booze got the unanimous vote every time—unless it was exam day.

On those days, the fear of failing would get me to class. I would walk into the crowded lecture hall, take a seat and try to use common sense to bluff my way through. However, this wasn't much good in technical classes like Music Appreciation 101 and Macroeconomics. Without actually doing the work, my grades were on an uncontrollable downhill slide.

After my exams, I would ease my pain by doing the usual: drinking hard and having sex with Ali. That was my prescription for low self-esteem, insecurity and the sense that I'd been abandoned in Wyoming. I hadn't heard from Uncle Lawrence since departing Kansas City. I felt completely alone, cut off. Why not drink?

One day, my fear and insecurity came to a head in an ugly way. I had become friends with a guy named Kevin Scott, a good-looking, six-foot-three, 200 pound, all-American white kid who was attending UW on a track and field scholarship. Kevin was one of the coolest cats I'd ever met. He was laid back and was always down for a drink.

Kevin was born and raised in the small town of Powell, Wyoming—a city that, like most in the state, rarely saw black people. So when I let Kevin convince me to drive home with him for a long weekend, I was a bit apprehensive. I had been to another small city in Wyoming during the fall semester and been stared at everywhere I went. I came to the conclusion that Wyoming isn't a preferred vacation destination for African-Americans. But, against my better judgment, I made the 7-hour drive with my friend.

When we arrived in Powell late Thursday night, Kevin took me to meet his mother. Her house would become our home base for our short trip. The next night, Friday, the games began. We went to one of Kevin's friend's homes to drink and hang out. His friend came from a rich family and their house was one of the most beautiful I had ever set foot in. They had a bar with a pool table! We sat around for a while, drinking beer and shooting pool, before leaving for a party at someone else's house.

I felt extremely uncomfortable at the party because there was nobody who looked like me. I also remembered that Wyoming was a state where everybody carried a gun. Knowing the effect that alcohol can have on people, I was afraid that one of the white guys would have too much to drink, lose his inhibitions, and start acting on his racial prejudice.

I guess my uneasiness got the best of me, because before I knew it, I was the one drunk and acting like a fool. The last thing I remember that night was drinking from a bottle of vodka like it was water and someone saying, "Either this dude can drink or he's going to be one fucked-up motherfucker!"

The next morning I woke up with dried puke all over my face, neck and clothes. The backs of my forearms were bloody and cut, and I was still drunk. Then, I started to hear the stories.

Kevin told me that I had been telling everybody I was a member of the Crips, I had an AK-47 and I wasn't afraid to kill anybody. He said I had been cursing and screaming and telling people I would "mess" them up. That is, until I passed out. Not long afterwards, I began to puke and gag on my own vomit. Some of the guys took me outside and sat me in a lawn chair on a gravel driveway. It wasn't long before I fell out of the chair and started crawling, commando-style, on the gravel, which explained the cuts on my forearms. Once I stopped puking, they brought me in out of the cold and laid me on the floor on my stomach, just in case I started to puke again.

I'd made an ass of myself and played into every black stereotype there was. I was humiliated and couldn't wait to leave.

Academic Suspension

I spent most of the rest of the semester with Ali. We did everything together, from shooting hoops and playing tennis to rock climbing and hiking the rock formations of Vedauwoo in the Medicine Bow National Forest. Being with her made me forget how much I was in the process of screwing up my life. But as the semester came to a close, I worried about our future together.

During all my activities with Ali, the one thing I failed to do was pay attention to my studies. I had promised Uncle Lawrence and my mom that I would improve my G.P.A. I did. I went from a 1.0 GPA to two Cs and two Ds—a 1.5 G.P.A. That wasn't going to cut it. I was no longer on academic probation; I was now on academic suspension. The only way I would be allowed to come back to school the next year was to successfully petition for a reprieve of the suspension and to find several thousand dollars to pay off the outstanding balance of my fees not covered by financial aid. If I couldn't come up with the money, the petition process wouldn't matter.

My last day in Laramie was a beautiful May morning, and it was one of the saddest days of my life. I was headed back to Kansas City. I had nowhere else to go. Ali drove me to the train station in Denver and came inside to see me off. When the call for my train came over the loudspeaker, we embraced tightly while the tears flowed. There was no guarantee that we would ever see each other again.

Finally, last call had me running to get on board. I looked out the window as I found my seat. Our eyes locked as the train pulled away. When I could no longer see her, I lay down in my seat and the empty seat next to me and cried myself to sleep. I woke as the train approached Union Station in Kansas City. Nine months earlier I thought I had escaped the misery of my life here. Now I was back, and I had no idea how I would be able to break free again.

CHAPTER 8

UNDER THE INFLUENCE

Living again in Kansas City, I felt like a failure. For the first time in life, I had no idea what came next. After fifth grade, you go into sixth grade. But what do you do when you're an 18-year-old college dropout with no money, no prospects and an alcoholic drug-dealer as your only supporter? Trouble was on the horizon.

My mother came to pick me up that morning, and we walked through the train station parking lot to the maroon Mercury Monarch that belonged to her boyfriend. From there, it was back to his shanty. I despised that house. But I had no place else to go. The Childress family was no longer an option. David and I weren't really speaking. The Blankinship family was closed off to me. Other than the brief conversation about my poor grades, I'd only spoken with Uncle Lawrence once during my entire time in Laramie. Plus, the wounded little boy inside me didn't want to ask him for help. I felt like I had let him down.

The house was even more despicable than I had remembered. My mother's boyfriend was no longer a simple pothead. He was a full-blown crackhead, and my mother was his pusher. Even my brother had become hardened. I knew this was not where I belonged. I just didn't know what I was going to do or how I was going to do it.

Des Moines, Again

A few days after I arrived, my mother said she was taking a trip to Des Moines and wanted me to accompany her. After my experience in King Park back in early January, I had no desire to ever see Des Moines again. But my mother really wanted me to ride with her. She promised a quick trip—in and out. So I agreed.

During the trip, I learned the extent of her drug dealing. Because Kansas City was a larger city than Des Moines and marijuana was more readily available, it was cheaper. My mother would buy pot in Kansas City and take it to Des Moines where demand was over the top. Buy low, sell high. It was Economics 101 put into practice.

Upon arriving in Des Moines, she drove us to an apartment community called Oakridge. We went to a door and knocked. A guy I'd never seen before answered. "What's up Aunt T?" he said with a warm grin. He led us up the stairs to the living room. My mother introduced me to the young man as her son and we exchanged greetings.

Then, they started talking about what was going on in the streets, things that I wanted nothing to do with. Finally, he said, "You got that bud Aunt T?" My mother immediately tried to redirect the conversation, "Where's Cameron?" she asked. This was insulting. I knew my mother smoked weed. I had always known. She knew that I knew. This was more of her delusional, "If I don't admit it, it doesn't really happen" thinking. What I didn't know at the time was that he was referring to weed to be distributed as well.

Cameron was my slightly younger cousin and the son of my mother's sister, Jackie, who passed away ten years prior.

"I don't know," the guy responded. "He should be here sometime today."

Throughout the time we were there, a lot of people came in and out of that apartment. They were all smoking weed and using vulgar language. It was evident this place was a drug house and the environment made me uncomfortable. I wasn't exactly sure why we were there, but I wanted to get out of there a quickly as possible.

As the day wore on and my mother waited on Cameron, I sat on a couch trying to be patient. In reality, I was nervous and fidgety. My mother never mentioned when we were leaving and I was afraid to ask her.

Finally, it got so late that I fell asleep on the couch sitting up. My mother, sitting on the other end of the couch, did the same. It wasn't until the next morning after we woke that Cameron had arrived. Despite everything, it was good to see him. He had a smile that would light up a room. We hugged and began to laugh because the mere sight of each other brought back great childhood memories.

Then he and my mother disappeared into another room. As always, this was my mother trying to hide her drug use, but I wasn't stupid. When she and Cameron came out I could tell they were both high. Finally, I was agitated. I was in somebody else's place. There was drug use going on and I was not comfortable with the situation. So, I found the courage to speak up.

"Mom, when are we leaving?" I said.

"A little bit later," she responded.

Several days later, we were still in that awful apartment. During that time, Cameron would come and go many times. I finally figured out that my mother was running weed from Kansas City and Cameron was selling it. He kept dropping off the cash he'd gotten for the weed he sold and would pick up more from her to sell. It became clear that we weren't going anywhere until all of my mother's drugs were sold.

Finally, fix or six days after we arrived, we got back in the car and began the drive back to Kansas City. I was in despair. This wasn't the kind of life I envisioned. But I had no money, no job and no place to live. The only thing that had given me any hope for the future had been my relationship with Ali, and that was likely gone for good.

During the drive home, I started to weep. "What's wrong?" my mother asked with concern. I told her how much I missed Ali and how much I wanted to go back to school. I'd messed up badly with my grades, but that didn't mean I didn't want to get my education. I sobbed furiously.

My tough-as-nails mother consoled me. "Son, don't worry. Everything is going to be okay. I'm going to make sure you get back to school," she said with conviction. She laid my head in her lap and comforted me as she drove.

A Tired, Broken Life

Despite her words, it was clear to me that everything was not going to be okay. My mother had become a full-fledged drug dealer, not someone just hustling a bag of weed here and there. She was crossing state lines with every ounce she could buy—and eventually, sell. How did she get to such a place?

Well, for 35 years life had beaten her up. She and her boys were living in the home of a man she didn't love or respect because she didn't feel she could make it on her own. She was tired and broken and believed money was the answer to her problems, just as I did. Drugs were the quick means to money and the money gave her a sense that she could stand on her own without having to beg for help or sell herself to some man.

Yes, she was doing it for herself. But she was doing it for my brother and me, too. During the drive back to Kansas City, I fell asleep in her lap. I could tell it hurt her to see me in pain. For all that she had done, she was the only one who never turned away from me, even when she had failed. Her love was the only constant I had.

Back in Kansas City, Ali and I would speak on the phone almost daily. Most of the time she would call me because I couldn't afford the long distance phone charges. Within weeks of the spring semester ending, Ali talked about moving to Denver for the summer. Her father agreed as long as she would be responsible for paying her own rent. She asked several friends to move with her, but none were willing. However, that didn't deter her.

Before long, Ali had found a job and an apartment. The apartment was a one bedroom, one bath off of South Parker Road on the Denver-Aurora city line. Her job would be as a night receptionist at an old hotel near Mile High Stadium, home of the Denver Broncos and the Arena Football League's Denver Dynamite, who housed their players at the hotel during the season.

Once she settled in, Ali asked if I would come visit her. I missed her more than I could stand. I would have done anything to be near her, especially without her father looking over her shoulder. However, I had two problems. One, I didn't have any money to buy a ticket. Two, I didn't have permission from my mother. I may have been 18, but since I was living with my mother I had to abide by her rules. So I was shocked when I asked her if I could go to Denver and she not only approved, but agreed to give me the money for a ticket. I thought that perhaps my grief during our drive back from Iowa had really gotten to her.

Ali was overjoyed. My plan was to stay in Denver for couple of weeks and return to Kansas City. And after that? If I was going to return to school, I needed $2,000 and to successfully convince the university that I wasn't a lost cause. I needed a miracle.

The Kirby

When I arrived in Denver in June of 1990, all was well. I was back in the arms of the one person who made everything okay. Our romance picked up right where it had left off. However, now, we were living together for the next couple of weeks, which was dangerous for two young people who didn't care about much more than our self-indulgent desires.

During my visit, however, Ali still had to work her 3pm-11pm shift at the hotel. Each day I would drive her to work, drop her off, and use her car to explore the city. Then I couldn't wait until it was time to pick her up and go back to her apartment. Being with her every day, all day—except when she was working—was great.

After about a week, we started discussing the proposition of me staying the entire summer. It sounded good to me. I had nothing going on in Kansas City. Everything I wanted in life was right there with her. But, we knew her father wouldn't go for it, so we in effect said, "What he doesn't know won't hurt him." As for my mother, when I asked her about staying, she was surprisingly okay with it. I couldn't have been more thrilled.

Now that I was staying in Colorado for two and a half more months, I needed a job. I began to scour the Denver Post's classified section every day, seeking only jobs that offered the greatest opportunity to make big bucks.

I answered an ad that offered the opportunity to make unlimited income and set my own hours. Income was what I needed and I'd never heard of such a thing before. This was before I really understood the idea that, "If it sounds too good to be true, it probably is." I was terribly young and naïve. So, I decided to call about the ad. During the phone conversation I was asked a few questions, and then was asked to attend an orientation the next day.

I arrived on time, dressed in my best clothes: trousers, a button down shirt, and the only tie I owned. A company representative took me and several other unsuspecting young men through the details of how people were making thousands of dollars per year. They talked about setting appointments and being paid for product demonstrations, so I knew it was some type of sales job. This made me feel uncomfortable because I had never really had a sales job. Worse, there seemed to be no guaranteed paycheck. Plus, I would need a car.

The second half of the orientation consisted of an introduction to the product: the crème de la crème of vacuum cleaners, The Kirby. This thing was the Ginsu before the Ginsu. I was so impressed by what it could do that I believed it would sell itself…right up until I found out that it cost $1,200. Who would pay that much for a vacuum? But based on the orientation, several sales associates were making a handsome living selling $1,200 vacuum cleaners. So, desperate for money and more excited than skeptical, my venture as a Kirby vacuum cleaner salesman began.

It didn't take long for my skepticism to become full-blown doubt. First, I came home that night with my $1,200 vacuum cleaner, excited to show Ali. I gave her the product demonstration and she was in awe of what the Kirby could do. Then she asked, "How much does that vacuum cost?"

"About $1,200."

"$1,200! Are you kidding me?" Her mouth and eyes wide, she started to giggle. "Who is going to buy a $1,200 vacuum?"

"There are plenty of people," I replied. "A lot of guys are making a lot of money selling these things. Once people see what it can do it's a no-brainer."

For the next week, in the summer heat, I went door-to-door in some of the most affluent neighborhoods in Denver offering to dry-foam shampoo the carpet in beautiful homes. I had no takers. I was a black kid in a tie, walking through some of the nicest neighborhoods in the city. I looked and felt out of place. When I did manage to set an appointment and give a product demonstration, the $1,200 price tag doomed any chance of a sale. Finally, I came to the realization that I was not going to be the next Kirby millionaire. I quit.

Still, I needed to make money. I couldn't make Ali pay the rent by herself. I went to a local grocery store—King Soopers—and completed an application. Within a day they hired me as a courtesy clerk. I would bag groceries, assist patrons in loading their purchases into their vehicles, and work to keep the parking lot free of shopping carts. It wasn't the most glamorous job, and at $4.25 per hour I wasn't going to get rich, but it was respectable and would allow me to pull my weight with living expenses.

End of Summer

Life was good. On our days off together, Ali and I would do different fun things in Denver, from Elitch Gardens Theme and Water Park to pari-mutuel wagering at the city's local dog track. We were two teenagers who didn't know what we didn't know but enjoyed the blindness of our love.

As the summer played out, my mother continued making her trips back and forth between Kansas City and Des Moines, trafficking marijuana. But in 1990 the fastest money on the streets was in cocaine. The street value of cocaine to marijuana was approximately five to one at that time, and cocaine sold much more quickly than marijuana because its high is fleeting, insatiable, and much more addictive.

Crack cocaine is the devil. One hit and it's like your body and mind become possessed by an evil spirit that does nothing but crave more of the drug, leaving you unable to focus on anything except your next high. My mother would learn all this firsthand from my father, a crack addict himself. She ran into him on one of her trips to Des Moines and told him that I needed financial help to get back to college. He asked her if she could get her hands on some crack because it was the fastest way to make the money she needed. Being an addict, I'm sure he had ulterior motives as well. In an instant, my mother went from primarily hustling marijuana to dealing crack. Her ex, the father of her children, was now her partner in crime.

My mother hadn't seen my father in over 10 years before their fateful encounter. His behavior, influenced heavily by his drug addiction, had been the reason we fled Des Moines. But in that chance meeting they began to rekindle their past relationship. My father was living with his mother and he invited my mother to stay at her house. His mother loved my mother. She knew the hell that my father had put her through over the years because of his drug addiction and prison stints, and how he left her with two kids to care for on her own. My grandmother was no stranger to that. She raised nine kids on her own. So, she was happy to help make amends.

While I spent my summer of love in Denver, my mother was on a high-octane mission to get paid going back and forth between Des Moines and Kansas City. Montez—who had one year of high school remaining—was left to live with my mother's crack addict ex-boyfriend whom she had suddenly left for my father.

But all good things come to an end, and so it was with my summer with Ali. The lease on the apartment ended, and it was time to move forward. The reality was as hard as a smack in the face. I was not returning to the University of Wyoming. I didn't have the money. Once again, I was headed home—this time to Des Moines, my mother's new home base. I didn't want to go but I had no choice.

Despite this depressing state of affairs, the past three months with Ali in Denver had been the best of my life. We had created a life together. We both had jobs and got to come home every night to each other. With her, I felt secure. My binge drinking had ceased. I didn't want the summer to end because, just like in May, Ali and I were going in different directions with no promise of seeing each other anytime soon.

In days, she would begin her freshman year at UW. She had plans for her life. But my life had come to a stop. I had nothing in front of me. No goals. No aspirations. No hope. Ali and I packed her car full of her belongings and she drove me to the Greyhound station. The tears flowed. I was terrified that once she started college she would find a new boy to replace me. Out with the old, in with the new.

At the bus station, we couldn't stop hugging, even after the final call for the Des Moines bus came. I grabbed my duffel bag full of clothes, gave Ali one final hug and kiss, and boarded the bus. I stared out the window and waved as the bus pulled away.

Bitter Reunion

The bus pulled up to the Des Moines station. As I descended the steps to exit the bus, I saw my mother, and next to her, my father. The tension was thick.

"Hey Mom," I said as I embraced her. I didn't know what to expect from my dad. Luckily, he spoke first as he reached out and hugged me.

"Hey son," he said as he squeezed me tightly.

All I could think was, "Where do you get off calling me 'son'?"

"How you doin'?" I said evenly.

"Good. How are you?" I didn't know whether to talk to him or try to fight him. I wanted to reply with a bitter, ironic, "How do you think I am? For 19 years, you've been M.I.A. I needed you. We needed you. What's your problem?" It took everything I had to maintain self-control and give him any respect. He deserved none.

In the calmest manner possible I responded, "I'm doing all right." I wasn't, of course. My life was off the tracks and I needed help. But I didn't want his.

I loaded my bag into the car and we made our way to my grandmother's house where, my father was forced to live. In his 36 years of life, he had accomplished nothing. He was a crack addict who had abandoned his woman and the two children they had created. I was too young to see that he was an older version of me. His father had done the same thing to him and his mother. He was simply carrying on the family tradition.

I hadn't seen my grandmother or any other members of my dad's family in more than a decade. But when we arrived at my grandmother's house, it didn't take long to rekindle the old bonds. My family welcomed me with open arms. Everyone said, "Boy, you look just like your daddy!" I didn't want to be like my daddy. What kind of man chooses drugs, alcohol and prison over his children? Forgiveness wasn't even a possibility.

My grandmother was another story. She was a sweet old lady tough enough to raise nine children on her own. Now retired, she spent each day drinking beer and playing solitaire at her kitchen table. She rarely left the house; as the matriarch of the Thomas family, her house was where family went when they had nowhere else to go. She called it the "flop house" because people would just come in, flop on the sofa or floor and never leave. She would bark about how she hated the fact that people treated her house that way, but she loved having her family around.

Now my mother and I were "flopping" with her, too. We just moved on in like we were paying rent and treated it like our own home. I was glad. The house was clean and I had family nearby. However, I wished that my little brother could have been with us.

My mother was still making her trips between Kansas City and Des Moines with my dad as her travel companion. Thank God! I didn't want anything to do with drugs. My dad didn't care; he was a veteran user and dealer who'd spent many of his 36 years incarcerated. How the relationship between my mother and father was going to work this time around was beyond me. Really, I didn't care. I was obsessed with getting myself back in school and back to Ali.

Drug Dealer

As the days passed, I grew more impatient. My life was not in Des Moines. However, I didn't see how I was ever going to get back to Wyoming. Money was not coming in fast enough. There were too many people sharing one pie. Plus, my mother was not hustling drugs at the street-level. She was relying on my cousins Aaron and Cameron and making money for her wasn't exactly their highest priority.

My mother's role in this little family crime syndicate was simply to run drugs and money back and forth between Des Moines and Kansas City. While this carried the greatest potential legal penalty, it was low visibility and low-risk. Most drug dealers are nickel and dime hustlers who are arrested during street-level retail transactions. For the most part, my mother sat at home waiting for my cousins to bring money to her.

Aaron and Cameron were taking the greatest risk and reaping the least reward, and it didn't take long before they figured out they were being used. Suddenly, money started coming up short. Unsold crack rocks were coming back smaller. Stories became more elaborate and farfetched. "The cops came and I had to throw the dope" was a popular one. "I lost the dope" was another.

There is no honor amongst thieves, and it became obvious to me that my cousins were skimming drugs and money off the top of what they gave my mother. They resented the fact that she was getting the most money and taking the least risk. This made me mad, because selfishly I wanted her to make enough cash so I could get back to Laramie. But that just wasn't happening quickly enough. She knew my cousins were stealing from her, but there was nothing she could really do. She was not willing to get in the streets and sell the drugs herself, and the financial losses were piling up.

Finally, I lost my patience and said to her, "Give me the drugs. I'll sell them."

In my mind, there was no way she was going to let that happen. She disciplined my brother and me when we used bad grammar; there was no way she was going to allow her son to be a drug dealer. But, to my shock, she handed me some crack cocaine. My cousin Aaron and my dad sat there looking on but said nothing. There I stood, holding crack in my hand for the first time. I had expected my mother to chastise me for the insinuation, not hand me drugs.

In that second, something profound shifted in my life. The little boy who had vowed never again to ask anyone for help was now in control of his own financial destiny. The mother who would kick our butts for being disobedient, and who would have put my brother and me in the hospital if we ever broke the law, had opened the door to the criminal underworld.

I couldn't turn back. I had to get enough money to get myself back to college and to the girl I loved. I made the single most critical choice I have ever made in my life: I closed my hand around the crack cocaine. I was a drug dealer.

Breaking the Rule

Of course, I had no idea what I was doing. It was like starting a new job in sales without a minute of training. Plus, unlike most jobs I had to watch out for the cops, street thugs who might try to rob me if they knew about the cash or drugs I was carrying, and snitches who were looking to cut deals with the cops in order to reduce their own prison sentences.

I was now part of the drug and criminal culture, and there were different rules. One mistake could cost you your life. My older cousin Aaron was my trainer. He wasn't new to the drug world. His older brother, Jamal (who had been so horrible to that poor addicted woman during my last visit to Des Moines) was one of the biggest dealers in the city, and Aaron learned everything he knew from Jamal.

The TNT Lounge, a local bar on the corner of Harding Road and Forest Avenue, was a hotspot for drug activity on the Westside. This is where Aaron would train me: how to identify someone looking for crack, how to talk to them and, ultimately, how to conduct the deal. Things happened quickly because everyone was afraid of being arrested. You had to be quick and inconspicuous. My training with Aaron lasted for a couple of weeks, and then he turned me loose on my own.

Each evening, Aaron and I would go to TNT to work the bar for sales. There were numerous drug dealers there at any given time, and the competition was intense. Some dealers would take less money for more product. Some buyers had established relationships with dealers and wouldn't buy from anyone else. The same sales principles you'd find in the business world—offering value and customer service, operated here. The only difference was the legality of the product being sold.

Competitive as I was, I hated when another dealer made a sale in front of me. I felt like I should make every sale. In an effort to beat the other dealers to the buyers, I broke a cardinal rule—a rule that my father, of all people, told me not to break. "Don't be standing on that corner outside that bar selling anything," he said. "The police are always watching that corner."

I didn't listen. In my overzealousness, I decided to stand outside the bar on the corner and conduct transactions. The police were watching with night vision binoculars and saw everything. Seconds after I made a deal, the cops swarmed the corner where my cousin and I were standing. Because my cousin had been around the drug scene longer than me, when he saw the police coming he ran and escaped arrest. I froze. I wasn't used to running from the cops.

Aaron got away and quickly found a phone and called my grandma's house to tell my mother and father I had been arrested. My grandma only lived a three-minute drive away from the bar, so my father jumped into the car and raced to the scene where I was being detained and the police were conducting their investigation. He had barely put the car in park before he jumped out, screaming, "Hey! What's going on?"

"Sir! Back up! Back up!" an officer shouted at my dad.

"That's my son!" my dad shouted at the officer. Two other officers at the scene began to restrain him. He began shouting, "Let me go! That's my son!" He was quite aggressive and the officers wrestled him to the ground while he screamed obscenities. That night both my dad and I wound up arrested and hauled down to the city jail in the same paddy wagon.

I'm not sure what I would have done had my father not been there on that ride with me to jail. I was scared. I had never been to jail. He knew that. Being that this wasn't his first rodeo, he knew the charges he would face for obstruction would be minimal. He also wasn't afraid of jail or prison. He had made a decision: he wasn't going to let me go to jail by myself. As messed up as that may sound, that was the best way my father knew how to show me he loved me. That was all he had.

We spent the night in the city jail. He cracked jokes and kept me preoccupied so I didn't break down. Meanwhile, I was scared. I had no idea what to expect. Early the next morning, we were both taken to court and formally charged by a judge. We were then released after agreeing to appear at a formal arraignment.

My head was spinning. In three weeks I had gone from never having been in real trouble to being arrested and charged with possession of a controlled substance with the intent to deliver. I didn't even know what the consequences were until I got the paperwork releasing me. My crime, I found out, was punishable by up to ten years in prison. My life flashed before my eyes.

I needed to get out of this city. But how would I do that now? I had a case pending in the county courts and I couldn't go anywhere until it was resolved. One possible resolution would send me to prison.

Facing the Music

After being released from jail I became a hermit of sorts. I hibernated at my grandmother's house. I woke each morning hoping that my legal problems were only a nightmare. Yet it would quickly register that they were real.

In short order, my life had turned into an oncoming train wreck. How do you go from a college student living with the love of your life to facing prison? It just didn't make sense. I couldn't understand how things had gotten so bad so fast. All I'd wanted was to get enough money to get out of town and back in school.

Several weeks later, I had my first court hearing. It was a preliminary hearing; I would be arraigned, enter a plea and be assigned legal representation from the Polk County Public Defender's Office. Bob Rigg was the attorney assigned to represent me. Bob was a tall, calm, brown-haired, brown-eyed, well-dressed white man. He briefed me on the structure of my hearing and told me I would be entering a plea of not guilty.

The judge called the court to order and my case was called up from the docket. "The state of Iowa versus Frank Eugene Thomas, Jr. in violation of Iowa penal code section 204.401(1)(a) possession of a controlled substance with the intent to deliver," the court clerk said.

"How do you plead?" the judge asked.

"Not guilty, your honor," I answered.

The judge went on to record the plea and scheduled the next hearing date.

After the hearing, Mr. Rigg told me how the process would unfold.

"Do you think I'm going to end up sentenced to prison?" I asked, trying to keep my voice from shaking.

"Frank, I can't make any promises to you," he said. "But, if you plead the case out you'll probably end up with probation, given you've never been arrested before and have no criminal record. However, the judge has the ultimate sentencing power. We'll see."

When I left the courtroom, I breathed a little bit easier. The possibility of probation gave me hope that I could still get out of Des Moines. But I still faced the same brick wall: with no money to my name I wasn't going anywhere. I had to get my ducks in a row, and the instant I was given permission to leave, I would be on the first thing smoking out of town.

After the hearing, Ali was the first person I called. She was happy to hear some positive news. My ordeal had been shocking to her. Then she said that she had some news for me.

"I'm thinking of moving to San Diego after Christmas to live with my sister," she said. "I talked with my Dad and told him I wanted to go out there and establish residency so I can attend San Diego State. He was cool with it. Would you come?"

I laughed. "I was willing to live in Wyoming because you were there. Now you want to twist my arm and have me go to sunny San Diego? Never!" I exclaimed. She laughed with me. "I've never been to California," I continued, "but anywhere is better than this place. I'm there!"

Just like that, our plans were set. If I could get out of the mess I'd created I was moving to San Diego with Ali. We said our goodbyes and I hung up. Now I just had to figure a way out of the fiasco I was in.

CHAPTER 9

CALIFORNIA DREAMIN'

Trouble was, things hadn't changed much. My mom was dragging her feet in helping me get out of town. So I made an agonizing decision: if I was ever going to get out of Des Moines, I had to take the risk and deal on the streets again.

To say I was cautious is an acute minimization. I couldn't afford one mistake. If I got caught, I knew I would end up in prison for a long time. I'd also have to go back to the scene of my arrest, the TNT Lounge. This time I couldn't take the risk of going outside the bar to make sales. I had to be patient and let the buyers come to me. Patience wasn't one of my strengths, but the stakes were too high for me to do anything else.

As luck would have it, sales started rolling in. Each day, I got more comfortable with the process of dealing, using my personality and ability to connect with people to my advantage. Before long, I had established my own clientele. Some users would come into the bar and be bombarded by several dealers at once, but they were only interested in buying from me. What was once a fear was now an exhilarating rush of adrenaline. I was making money faster than I had ever dreamed possible. My confidence in dealing drugs was growing.

Every night at the end of the night, I would take the remaining drugs and whatever money I made and give them to my mother. However, after several weeks, I began to notice something. Not only hadn't we made any more money, it seemed to be disappearing. We were barely treading water. This was not good. The streets were dangerous, and I was putting my future on the line every time I made a deal. The money was just not adding up, and I had a pretty good idea why.

Aaron was still skimming drugs and money off the top. He would leave the house with rock cocaine with a street value of $400 and return with $150 in cash and rocks with a street value of $100. When I would question where the money and supply had gone, he always had an excuse.

My father made the problem worse. As well as my mother tried to hide the drugs and money from him, he'd find them, take my grandmother's car, and go on multi-day binges. By the time my mother found him, he had always smoked all the drugs and used the cash to buy more.

Eventually my mother even began dipping into the money to buy clothes and jewelry. One afternoon, my frustration came to a head. My mom and I got in a huge fight over money. We were in the upstairs bedroom my mom and dad shared.

"You're wasting our fucking money!" I shouted. "I'm trying to get the fuck out of here! I can't stand it here!"

"You need to lower your motherfucking voice speaking to me!" she yelled back. "Who the fuck do you think you're talking to, boy?"

Aaron and my dad jumped in to stop us.

"I'm done!" I screamed. "I don't need you! I can do it on my own! I don't need any-motherfucking-body!" I turned, ran down the stairs and stormed out. I knew I had to get out of that awful place.

The Urban Jungle

This was the early 1990s, when crack cocaine and urban drug violence were part of the culture, glamorized in music and movies. Rap artists like NWA, Ice Cube, Tupac, MC Eiht and Too Short played significant roles in the way I interacted with society. The pain of being a poor black male was reflected in the music and lyrics of my favorite songs. These artists spoke directly to me because we shared the same struggles. Their songs became the manifestos by which I lived.

I became extremely angry, a walking contradiction. Inside of me was still the good kid, smart and a hard worker. I just needed a hand to reach my potential. But once Uncle Lawrence let go of my hand and the Childress family was no longer an influence in my life, everything positive had disappeared. I fell victim to the plague of the drug world.

On the streets of Des Moines, I adapted quickly. Money was the name of the game. Because my cousin Jamal was a feared drug dealer, I got respect that the average dealer wouldn't have gotten. Drug dealers got robbed every day, but the thugs gave me a pass. They knew if they messed with me, they would have to mess with "Big J" and the consequences wouldn't be nice.

With Uncle Lawrence out of my life, my role models became those who were ghetto fabulous. Jamal filled the void. He and I weren't particularly close, but he was the benchmark for success on the streets in our family. Jamal rolled with people who had Des Moines's drug trafficking locked down. If Jamal didn't have drugs, the city was pretty much dry. People like my mother would take advantage of these dry conditions because her supplier was in Kansas City.

Jamal would laugh and talk about how my other cousins were two-bit hustlers. "These niggas out here hustlin' for tennis shoes," he'd say. "They don't know nothin' about makin' money. I started from nothing. Within six months I made my first 5 Gs." Then he'd laugh. I'd listen and make mental notes.

As I got deeper and deeper into the drug trade, my mind and heart began to change, too. Chasing after the fast money became a game to me, a rush. I still had every intention of getting out of Des Moines, but I'd never felt the sense of power that fast money gave me. Jamal made $5,000 in six months. I made $5,000 in three months. I would be the first person awake in the entire city in order to make money. I would be the last one sleep at night, too.

I had money on the brain. It was all I cared about. I was convinced that it solved every problem I could ever have. Those days as a kid growing up without food, working utilities, or Christmas gifts? Those were in the past. Life was different with money. The more money I made, the more I thought, "I don't need help from anyone. " I'd finally found the key to feeling good about who I was, and nothing had ever felt better.

As great as it felt to have money, the thought of potentially losing my life for being in the wrong place at the wrong time was scary. On two different occasions I was within five feet of a shootout. On a third occasion, in the dead of winter, I was playing darts near the front door of the TNT Lounge with Jamal. All of the sudden, the front door opened and in walked in a black man in a long black goose down coat with a hood. I couldn't tell who it was at first. He walked straight toward me and my cousin, pulled out a sawed-off double barrel shotgun with a pistol grip handle, and pointed it directly at us. My hands went up immediately. I knew who it was.

"C., put the gun down," my cousin said calmly.

"Yeah, motherfucka!" he said. "Caught ya' slippin', nigga!"

I was shaking. C. was a Crip that Jamal used to run with, but he'd gotten so strung out on drugs, that Jamal distanced himself from him. He was one of those crazy dudes who didn't care about anything and feared nothing. Prison and death didn't faze him. Every time I saw him before that evening I'd always tried to avoid him. I could tell he wasn't playing with a full deck. Crazy ran in his family too—something that was confirmed a couple of years later when his brother was indicted for a gruesome double murder in a small farm community outside of Des Moines.

"C., come on man. Quit playin'," Jamal said.

C. started to smile and back up. "Watch your back, nigga," he warned, then lowered the gun and took off out the front door.

Money Addict

The money kept flowing. Although I didn't recognize it at the time, I came to realize that it didn't matter whether you were using drugs or selling drugs, you became an addict. I was no different. As badly as I wanted to get out of Des Moines, the money had a hold on me.

Meanwhile, Ali moved to San Diego permanently right after Christmas 1990. In late January 1991, I flew to San Diego to visit her. When I landed at San Diego International Airport, the temperature was in the low 70s. It was the first time I had ever seen a palm tree.

Ali was waiting at the arrival gate. Seeing her suddenly made everything in my life okay. We got into her car and took a drive around the city. I was in awe of the beauty. I couldn't help but notice how many successful looking African-Americans there were. I wasn't used to that. With the exception of my Uncle Lawrence, most of the African-Americans I knew at that time were struggling to survive. I desperately wanted to leave that world behind.

That day as we drove around I was struck with the overwhelming sense that California was where my dreams were going to come true. The Bible says in the book of Proverbs, "Where there is no vision, the people perish." That day I received a vision for my life and it had California written all over it.

Sadly, my trip was over quickly and I found myself back in Des Moines. I continued to hustle. My sentencing was set for Wednesday, February 20, 1991 and I was hoping for the best.

When I showed up for court, I was nervous. I had no idea what was going to happen. I was trying to think positively and take solace in what my cousin Jamal told me: "Don't worry. It's your first offense," he said. "Typically, you get probation on your first offense. Plus, you said the judge presiding over your case is Judge Fenton. He's a softy." I could only hope that he was right.

As I entered the courtroom, I saw Mr. Rigg, my attorney.

"Frank, how are you?" he said.

"Okay, I guess."

"Here's the deal. In exchange for a guilty plea, the D.A. is going to recommend a 10-year prison sentence." I suddenly felt faint, but he continued to speak.

"However, he is recommending the prison sentence be suspended and that you be placed on two years of supervised probation. You would also be given a deferred judgment."

"What's a deferred judgment?"

"If you successfully complete your probation without getting into any further trouble, the conviction would be expunged from your record as though it never occurred," he said. "Frank, this would be great for you. The courts don't give deferred judgments every day."

I didn't know why I was getting such a break, but I wasn't about to look a gift horse in the mouth.

"I will gladly take a deferred judgment. Mr. Rigg," I said.

This was the opportunity I needed to get my life on track for good.

The hearing went exactly as Mr. Rigg had said it would. I walked out of the courtroom feeling like I'd gotten my life back—with conditions. However, they were conditions I knew I could live up to. I was instructed to contact the County Department of Probation office within 48 hours to set up an appointment to meet with a probation officer. Once I did that, I'd be on my way to Southern California within a week.

I raced home to my grandmother's house and told everyone the news. Then I called Ali. She was as excited as I was about the news. After our call, I called the Department of Probation to schedule my appointment with my assigned officer. I didn't want to waste a second. I was ready to go, and the sooner the better.

Probation

My appointment at the Department of Probation was scheduled for the following week. Everything seemed to be going according to plan. I could only hope that they would agree to transfer my probation to California.

At the probation office, an African-American woman in her mid-to-late thirties stepped out of the hallway and said "Frank Thomas?" I stood up and reached my hand out to shake hers, but it was met by an awkward pause. Apparently, shaking hands with probationers was not protocol. Reluctantly, she reached out and shook my hand.

"Lynelle Hawthorne," she said. I could tell right away that Ms. Hawthorne was the type you didn't cross. And in no way did I plan to get on her bad side.

We walked down the long hallway to her office, where I was told to take a seat. She rustled through a stack of paperwork on her desk then pulled out a file. She immediately started asking questions, which I answered succinctly and honestly. Then she asked, "What drugs?"

"Pardon me?"

"What drugs do you do?" she said, never raising her eyes to look at me.

"I don't do drugs, ma'am." Now she raised her head from the file and locked her eyes on mine.

"Don't lie to me," she said. "I'm going to make you drop today and it won't be good if you come up dirty. So, I'm going to ask you again. What drugs do you do?" Obviously, many of her charges had lied to her over the years.

"I do not do drugs, ma'am," I said. "I've never done a drug in my life."

She went into her desk drawer and pulled out a clear cup with a white top, obviously used for collecting urine samples. "Follow me," she snapped.

I followed. She led me to a bathroom and called for one of the nearby male probation officers. She handed me the cup and I stepped into the bathroom with the officer behind me. After filling the cup I twisted the lid on it tightly and handed it to him. Then I washed my hands. We marched silently back to Ms. Hawthorne's office where the grilling continued.

"I noticed you wanted to transfer your probation to California," she said. "Who do you know there?"

"My girlfriend."

She asked me questions about Ali: what she did for a living, her address, and so on.

Twenty minutes later, the guard knocked on Ms. Hawthorne's door. "He's clean," he said simply. She nodded. She then gave me special instructions about transferring my probation to California. I listened intently. Finally, she said, "Do you have any questions?"

"No. I don't think so."

"Okay. Well, good luck in California," She said. I thanked her for her time, left the office and headed home. California, here I come!

California Bliss

I raced back to my grandmother's house. When I walked in the door, my grandma was sitting there drinking beer and playing solitaire like always. "I got the green light, Grandma," I crowed. "I'm headed to Cali."

"Well, you go 'head wit yo bad self!" she said as we both laughed. I couldn't wait to call Ali and tell her.

I began to pack my things, but before I left I knew I had to make up with my mother for the fight we had and for leaving home that cold winter night three years earlier. But it wasn't easy. By this time, she was a stone cold drug dealer, and her obsession with that lifestyle had further soured our relationship. Dealing changes you, and you can't escape it. If you don't totally embody the role, the streets will sniff you out. And the addiction to the money is insatiable. Almost no one quits selling drugs just because they want to. Most get put out because they get caught. Drug dealing is a desperate act of desperate people, and my mother and I were no different. The difference was that I had been busted and was leaving it behind. She couldn't. She had nothing else.

In my final minutes before leaving for the airport, I stood at the bottom of the stairs of my grandmother's two-story house and called for my mom. As she walked down the stairs, I could feel the heartbreak. "I'm leaving now,

Mom," I said. She hugged me and started to sob. She hugged me tighter than I could remember. It was a hug that said I'm sorry. I'm sorry for all of the pain. I'm sorry for relying on you as a child when you should have been able to rely on me. I'm sorry for teaching you the wrong things. I'm sorry for giving up on you and your brother.

But more than anything the hug said I love you. As my mother wept in my arms, I couldn't do anything but hold her. I would have done anything to take away all the pain that she'd ever felt. But I couldn't. I could only tell her, "It's okay. I love you too." And as she pulled herself together, I picked up my bags near the door and was on my way.

I was 19 years old, and it was time for me to go. The place that I would call home from this day forward would be built on my own terms. One thing was certain: drugs had no place in that life. I would do it the right way.

I arrived in beautiful San Diego, California. It was as beautiful as I'd remembered, but the best part about it was being with Ali again. I moved in with her, her sister, and her sister's boyfriend. It was a rather cozy arrangement, but it didn't matter. My move represented a new beginning and I was excited about the possibilities. Next, I needed employment.

At this time, in 1991, the U.S. military was in the middle of the Persian Gulf War and our country was in a deep recession. For the first time in my life I'd become aware of the effects of an economic downturn. They'd happened before, when I was a kid, but I'd had no real understanding of their impact. Now that I was supporting myself, I could feel the direct impact of the economic decline.

I began to look for work. Ali had a job working at a small retail store in the Horton Plaza in downtown San Diego's Gaslamp Quarter before I had arrived. I didn't relish the idea of being the only one of the four of us not bringing home a paycheck. Sitting at home made me feel like less than a man. Plus, I knew the money I had made from dealing drugs wouldn't last forever.

I also learned very quickly that Southern California was not the place to be without a car. I needed some reliable transportation. Several dealerships into my hunt, I found my dream car: a blue 1987 Suzuki Samurai soft-top convertible. It had Southern California written all over it.

Life in San Diego was bliss. Ali and I would spend time at the beach playing in the sand and walking along the Mission Beach boardwalk each week-end. We were young, in love and didn't have a care in the world. However, my lack of employment was a problem. I wouldn't be able to make it long without a job. Plus, finding gainful employment was a major condition of my proba-tion.

Full Circle

In late April 1991, I still hadn't found a job. But things would change in an instant. I received a message from my mother, who told me that I had been summoned to appear at a deposition in Kansas City at the end of the month related to the car accident four years earlier.

That trip, as I've already chronicled, led to my ultimate nightmare: being arrested and charged for drugs that belonged to my mother. Now, I was thrust back into the system. But this time, chances were that I would never escape.

CHAPTER 10

BETRAYED

The arresting officers took me to the Polk County Jail where I was booked and taken to an interrogation room. As I sat there in disbelief, the door opened. In came two detectives who sat down across the table from me. One of them began to read me my Miranda rights again, and then looked at me with a smirk. "You're fucked, man," he said. "You're going down for a long time unless you make it easy on yourself."

"I'm innocent," I said. Both detectives laughed as if that was the funniest thing they had ever heard.

"Innocent? We find an ounce of crack cocaine packaged and ready to go and several thousand dollars in the glove compartment of your car and you're innocent? Bullshit! You're fucking guilty and you know it!"

"I didn't do anything wrong!"

"You're facing federal time unless you to talk," the detective said. "You give us some information and we'll see what we can do to lessen the sting for you." He stared, waiting for me to reply.

"I don't know anything," I said. "I didn't do anything." I really didn't have anything to tell him. They tried several dirty tactics to try and get me to speak about things I had no idea about. They asked me questions I didn't have answers to. "I don't know," I responded again and again. After an hour, the interrogation ended and I was taken to a cell.

I sat there, shaken. I had no idea what was going on. When a guard came by, I asked if I could make a phone call. Several minutes later, he led me to a phone, where I placed a collect call to my grandma's house.

My aunt Kim answered the phone.

"Aunt Kim?" I said. "Where's my mom?"

"She's not here."

"Where is she?"

"She's trying to get you and your dad out right now." I told her to tell my mom to do whatever she could to get me out of here. There was nothing else to say. I hung up and the guard escorted me back to my cell. I sat there cold, scared and in shock of what just happened.

Later that evening, I was startled by the sound of the guards opening my cell door. "You made bail," one of them said. Thank God. The first person I needed to see was my mother. She was going to have to tell the truth and make this situation right.

My mom and dad were waiting for me in the lobby of the Polk County Jail. I was furious, but I knew the jail lobby wasn't the place to begin my rant. Once we got to the car, I couldn't hold my tongue.

"You need to tell the truth!" I shouted.

"Relax," she said. "We're going to work everything out." This led me to believe she was going to do the right thing and turn herself in—at least for a minute. "For the time being, you need to get out of here and cool off. Let's get you back to San Diego until we can work this thing out."

As long as she tells the truth, I thought, I should be fine. I had an arraignment scheduled for the first week in June and I wanted this situation to be resolved before then so I could move on with my life.

Within a day, I was on a plane back to San Diego. I shared everything that had happened with Ali, and she consoled me. I was devastated. I couldn't believe that this was happening. But, I was naively hopeful because I was confident that my mother would stand up and tell the truth rather than let her son pay for her crimes.

From Bad to Worse

A couple of days later, when I called my grandma's house and I asked to speak with my mother, I was told she wasn't there. Over the next few days, it became clear that she was avoiding me. She knew I was going to keep asking her to tell the police truth that the drugs found in my car were hers. A sick feeling was growing in the pit of my stomach.

To make matters worse, the police had come by Grandma's house looking for me. Unbeknownst to me, by not notifying my probation officer within 48 hours of being arrested, I was in violation of the terms and conditions of my probation. There was a warrant out for my arrest! Things had gone from bad to worse. I had thought that as long as I completed my monthly report and notified my probation officer about what had happened, I was in full compliance. But that's not how it worked. I was now a fugitive too.

My life was quickly falling apart. I was terrified that the authorities were going to come to San Diego, pick me up and extradite me back to Des Moines. I was advised by an attorney to stay in San Diego until my scheduled arraignment date, and turn myself in the day before. I tried to find some peace about what was happening, but it was impossible. Worst of all, it was becoming more and more clear that my mother was not going to do the right thing. She was going to sacrifice me to save herself. She had betrayed me.

June came, and I prepared to leave for Iowa to answer my probation violation charges. I hugged Ali with everything I had. We both hoped everything would be okay, and I would be home soon. But my intuition was giving me the sense that this was only going to get more ugly.

I arrived in Des Moines and my father picked me up from the airport. No sign of my mother. He immediately drove me to the Department of Probation where I surrendered to Ms. Hawthorne for my supposed probation violation. My dad told me my mom would bail me out as soon as my bond was set. When I walked into Ms. Hawthorne's office, I was immediately handcuffed. It had been only three months earlier that I had sat in her office, being placed on formal probation, thinking I would never return or find myself on the opposite side of the law ever again. Now, I was being arrested for violating that probation and facing a slew of new charges.

I was expected to take a drug test again. The results came back negative, just like before. Once Ms. Hawthorne was finished with me, one of the detectives who had interrogated me in the small room on the day I was arrested during the raid of my grandma's house was waiting to take me to the county jail. He grabbed my arm and led me to his car where he shoved me into the front seat. With my hands cuffed behind me, he fastened my seatbelt and slammed the door.

On the drive to the jail the detective was badgering me, telling me that I was finished and I should get ready to rot in prison for the rest of my life. I didn't say anything. He was trying to intimidate or provoke me, and I wasn't going to give him the satisfaction. I kept calm—until I was booked into jail and found out my bond had been set at $60,000.

I didn't have that kind of money and neither did my mother or anyone else I knew. I sat in my jail cell, wanting to cry my eyes out. But God forbid the other inmates saw me crying and thought I was soft. Who knew what they would try and do to me?

Betrayed

As soon as I had a chance to use the phone, I called my grandma's house. My mom answered.

"How ya doin'?" she said.

"How do you think I'm doin'? You need to get me outta here now!"

"I'm working on it," she said. "It's just going to take me a little time."

In that second, it clicked. I'd never been surer of anything. My mother had no intention of telling the truth. She never did. I felt like someone had punched me in the gut.

I knew, right then and there, that I was in the fight of my life. There was no way I going down for something I didn't do. With no one else to turn to, for the first time in my life, I prayed to God in earnest. I called out to God because every person I'd ever depended on in my life had failed me. I had come to the end of my reliance on others and to the end of myself. No one could save me. God was all I had left.

I was hopeful that my mother would at least get me out on bail. She said she would, and I desperately wanted to believe her. But why? She had lied to me so many times; why would this be different, especially when she had so much to lose? I was hoping for a miracle from someone who was incapable of performing one.

As I sat in my cell, every now and then I could hear a voice over the PA system calling the names of people who had made bail. Each time, I would sit up in my bunk, praying that the voice would call my name. But it never did. I would call my grandma's house and plead with my mother to get me out. Her response was always the same: "I'm working on it."

Finally, on the morning of my arraignment, her story changed.

"Would you rather get out on bail?" she said. "Or would you rather I use the money to hire an attorney? I can't do both." Now, it was clear: she had no intention of getting me out of jail.

I think she was expecting me to tell her I would rather have an attorney. But I said, "I would rather get out of jail." It was the wrong call. Only a good attorney could possibly help end this nightmare. If I was found guilty, no dollar amount could buy my freedom. However, her question obviously was a rhetorical one because she ignored my wishes and had already hired an attorney. I was going to trial for a crime I hadn't committed, and I knew that I might not be a free man again for a long time.

PART TWO

The Rise

CHAPTER 11

MY ONLY HOPE

My attorney was a man by the name of Mark Pennington. My mother had known Mark from her days working for the Polk County Attorney's Office. When he arrived at my arraignment hearing, I found out I was charged with one count of possession of an illegal substance with the intent to deliver, one count of possessing an illegal, unregistered firearm, and one count of failure to obtain a drug stamp identifying that proper taxes had been paid on the drugs in question.

The police had pinned everything on me. They were trying to make their case stronger because if I were convicted, they would look like heroes for taking another dealer and gun off the streets. Immediately, Mark advised me to plead not guilty to the charges. He also informed me that the probation violation hearing would be delayed until the resolution of the drug charges was complete.

Several days after the arraignment, Mark showed up at the county jail to meet with me and get the facts of the case. As we sat together in a room reserved for attorneys and their clients, he began to explain to me the severity of the charges. Panicked, I said, "I'm innocent, Mark! I'm innocent!"

He'd obviously heard these words before. "Frank you're facing some very serious charges," he said. "If convicted, in conjunction with the felony you're already on probation for, you could face a maximum of up to 60 years in prison."

"I'm innocent. Those were not my drugs!" I protested." They belonged to my mother!" But the drugs had been found in my car, and I was being held responsible. The truth just didn't matter.

As I tried to collect myself, 60 years kept flashing in my mind. Sixty years. I was 19. Sixty years in prison would be a death sentence. I was overwhelmed with fear. Finally, I asked, "Do you think you could get me a deal? For like ten years? I don't know if I can take the chance at fighting and losing. If I get 60 years, I'll be an old man by the time I get out!"

Mark gave me a serious look. "Frank, based on the facts, I think I can beat this case," he said.

"Mark, I'm too scared to take that chance. Can't you see if I can get a deal?" In my eyes going to trial was just too risky.

Mark sighed. "Ok, Frank. I'll see what I can do. But, I think I can beat this case!" Our meeting came to an end and I was sent back to my cell to deal with the news.

About a week and a half later, Mark came to the jail to meet with me. He looked grim as he gave me the news. "Frank, the District Attorney is not interested in giving you a deal," he said. "They think they have enough evidence to get a conviction."

I sat there, stunned. My life flashed before me. I didn't have a choice. The District Attorney wanted a fight. I would have to give him one because I was not pleading guilty to 60 years in prison for something I did not do. He wanted to nail me to the cross. Only God can help me now, I thought.

Turning to God

Mark left and I was taken back to my cell. I got on the floor and prayed until my knees gave out. From that day, I began to pray to God many times a day. I also began to read a Bible I'd found in the dayroom of the jail. The more I read and prayed, the more encouraged I began to feel.

Each day I would read more and then spend more time praying. Before long I started to feel hope. I felt myself slowly coming back to life. While I may have been physically incarcerated, I'd stopped allowing my mind and my spirit to be imprisoned. I started to gain the confidence that Mark had the day of our first meeting. Now I believed we were going to be able to beat this case, too.

One day I was sitting on the floor at the end of the hallway that housed the cells on my tier, reading my Bible. A gentleman who had been booked into the jail only a few days earlier walked up to me. I noticed that he had some very feminine qualities, and I got this weird feeling about him.

"My name is Luther." He stuck his hand out.

"I'm Frank," I responded apprehensively as I reached out to shake his hand.

"What are you reading Frank?" he inquired, as he invited himself to sit down right next to me. I knew he knew what I was reading. He had seen me carrying my Bible around.

"I'm reading my Bible."

"What book?"

"John."

Luther began to share some insight and knowledge with me about the book of John and the things of God. He went on to tell me that he was a preacher's kid and that he grew up in the church.

"Are you saved?" he asked suddenly.

"Saved? What do you mean?"

"Do you believe in your heart that Jesus Christ is the Son of God and that he died for the sins of the world and your salvation?"

"Yes, I do."

"Have you confessed it with your mouth?"

"No. But I believe."

"That's not enough, Frank. Would you like to be saved today?"

"Yes!"

On the spot, Luther led me in the Sinner's Prayer. I accepted Jesus Christ as my personal Lord and Savior. That day, a sense of peace that surpasses understanding overcame me. Luther and I began to read and pray together every day during our stay in the Polk County Jail. He was a divine appointment in my life.

Not long after all of this went down Ali arrived in Des Moines to support me. This meant everything; she had quit her job and dropped her life in San Diego for me. It seemed like with every challenge I had faced since I met her, she'd been there, faithful and without question. We talked every day on the phone and wrote letters, and she visited me as often as the rules would allow.

I told her that I had gotten saved but Ali wanted nothing to do with God. She would get upset with me when I even brought up His name. I didn't understand it. But she was not willing to hear anything I had to say about Him.

Even so, I kept praying and reading my Bible. I prayed for my freedom and that my relationship with Ali would grow deeper and with greater maturity. As my faith increased I told a couple of guys on my tier how confident I was that I was going to be freed. They laughed at me, but I held my head high. God knew I was innocent and I knew He was going to deliver me, not just from this physical prison, but from the prison of my sense of low self-worth.

As awful as my circumstances were, for the first time in my life I was at peace. Seems strange, doesn't it? But I didn't have to worry about where I was going to lay my head and how I was going to pay for it. I didn't have to worry about if I was going to eat. I didn't have to worry about anything but the fight. All I'd done for the first 19 years of my life was worry about surviving, and I didn't need to do that now. I didn't worry about fitting in, walking lightly in someone else's home, or about begging for help. I was incarcerated, but for the first time in my life I was free.

Happy Birthday

My trial was scheduled for early August, and on July 9, I celebrated my 20th birthday sitting in a jail cell. It was a tough day to be locked up. Ali came to visit me and all I wanted to do was be with her.

Later that evening, I was reading my Bible when I heard someone yell my name. I went into the dayroom to see what was going on. All the guys were crowded around the large window that overlooked the street below. "Yo, man!" someone yelled. "They out there for you!"

I went to the window and saw my brother, dad, mom and Ali holding up a sign that read, "Happy 20th Birthday Frank!" They had cupcakes with lit candles in their hands. I waved my arms to acknowledge that I could see them, and they sang "Happy Birthday". I've forgotten most of my birthdays. But that one I will never forget.

My trial date was approaching quickly, and as it did my prayers became more intense. I promised God that if He delivered me from this debacle, I would never touch drugs again. I wasn't negotiating; I would keep my promise regardless of whether I was vindicated or not. This experience had changed me. I walked into that jail an immature boy, but the experience of finding the Lord in the middle of my difficulties had transformed me. Now I was a man. I was no longer afraid of what lay ahead. I knew that I had the courage to face it, no matter what. But I never lost my faith that I would be exonerated.

My trial began on a warm, sunny Monday morning in August of 1991. So began a five-day stretch that would turn out to be the most riveting of my life. The spotlight was on me, a 20-year-old African-American male facing a three-count felony indictment that could put me away for what was virtually the rest of my life if convicted.

My only goal was to prove to a jury that I was innocent. I had gotten over the fact that the prosecution had accused and indicted the wrong person. That couldn't be changed. That truth was no longer a relevant part of the case. The only relevant issue, now, was working to be acquitted.

Unfortunately, the prosecution was out for blood. Their lead attorney was an ambitious up-and-comer named Jamie Bower, whose expertise was high profile cases dealing with drugs and gangs. The spotlight was also on him. To successfully prosecute a case of this magnitude would be a huge boost to his career.

My attorney, Mark Pennington, was an older, well-educated veteran. He was articulate and had tremendous charisma. When he spoke, he exuded confidence, mesmerizing people with his eloquence and the intelligence of his oration. Mark believed in my innocence and we were yoked together in the pursuit of justice. If the prosecutor lost the case, it would have been a blow to his ego and perhaps a career setback, nothing more. For Mark, failure would have been like consigning his own son to life behind bars. The stakes were personal for him.

The Trial Begins

The crucial process of jury selection played out, and after many hours, a jury was seated and its members took their oath. The trial was ready to begin, but it was late in the afternoon so the judge decided to adjourn until Tuesday morning. I went back to my cell and spent most of the evening in prayer, reading my Bible. I was sick with anxiety and needed time alone with God to calm my troubled soul. I didn't sleep very well that night. I wanted the process to be underway, the waiting to be over.

The next day, I arrived in the courtroom with my police escort and sat at the defense table. Mark was going over final details for the day's proceedings.

He looked at me with a smile. "Good morning, Frank."

"Good morning."

"How'd you sleep last night?"

"Not very well." I folded my hands and placed them on the table. Mark smiled.

"Hang in there." It took every ounce of strength I had to smile back. He had prepared me as best he could for how the trial would proceed, but it was still alien territory for me.

The judge entered the courtroom and called the proceedings to order. He gave a few simple instructions, and then it was time to pick up where things had ended the day before, with opening statements.

Mr. Bower, the prosecution's attorney, went first. He wasted no time unleashing a barrage of lies against me, portraying me as the scum of the earth. It took all my restraint to keep from screaming. If I had been a juror listening to him, I would have cast a guilty vote on the spot.

Like a prizefighter, Bower struck fast and hard, and held nothing back. I felt like I'd been knocked to the canvas without even getting a chance to throw a punch. My body was stiff. I was clinging onto the arms of my chair, white-knuckled. When the prosecutor finished his opening statement I was stunned and dazed.

The reality of the situation hit me hard. The truth wasn't going to set me free. The prosecution didn't care that I was innocent. I was their big fish, and they were going to do everything to put me away, truth be damned. My only hope was in the Lord and that my attorney was as good as he appeared to be.

Mark stood and wasted no time attacking the prosecution's case. His job was simple: poke holes in their evidence and assertions in order to create reasonable doubt in the jury's mind. He launched an all-out assault on the prosecution's claims. Where I'd been white-knuckling my chair in terror and anger, I was now gripping it to keep from jumping out and shouting, "Yeah!" When Mark ended his opening statement, he looked at me with a long hard stare that said, "I'm going the distance for you. I'll be the only one left standing in the end."

Now it was time to present evidence to the jury, and the prosecution went first. Bower called several witnesses to the stand. One of the prosecution's star witnesses was a detective who had helped to execute the search warrant, Kevin Frampton. Frampton took the stand and Bower questioned him about the sting operation and eventual raid at my grandma's house. Frampton testified that local law enforcement had police informants buy drugs from the house on several occasions in the period leading up to the raid. He stated where the drugs and gun were found in my car and house and other facts about the search warrant.

While the prosecution was examining its witness, Mark was listening intently. Occasionally, he would make a note. I sat breathing deeply, trying to stay calm, which was difficult when the witness told blatant lies about me. Finally, the prosecutor ended his examination of the witness, and Mark got his opportunity to cross-examine Mr. Frampton.

Star Performance

"Mr. Frampton, how many times did your police informant purchase drugs from the house on 18th Street?"

"Several times," replied Frampton.

"How many of those times did that informant purchase those drugs from the defendant?"

"Zero. None."

"Zero?"

"Yes. Zero." said the detective.

"Do you know why the informant never purchased drugs from my client?"

"No. Why?"

"The reason your informant never purchased drugs from my client is because my client didn't live in that house. He was over 1,700 miles away living in San Diego, California, during the entire time of your investigation. That's why detective."

Mark went on. "Isn't it true that my client was never identified at any point in time during your investigation as a suspect of interest or included in your affidavit to the judge to receive a search warrant for the house?"

"That's correct," the detective stated.

"Isn't it true also that your search warrant was for the premises and did not include the vehicles?" asked Mark.

"Yes. That's correct."

"And isn't true that when officers asked my client for permission to search his vehicle, he gave it to them willingly?"

"Yes," replied the detective.

"If my client was dealing drugs and had knowledge that drugs were in his car, do you think he would give you consent to search it without a warrant? Because I don't."

"It's possible," said the detective. "It happens more than you might think."

"So, when you searched the car, what did you find?"

"We found thirty grams of crack cocaine rocks that were cut and packaged for sale and several thousand dollars in cash," the detective replied.

"Were forensic tests performed on the packaging of the drugs and the gun?"

"Yes," said Frampton.

"Were my client's fingerprints lifted off of any of the evidence?"

"The results were inconclusive. We can't say no, his prints were not on either the drugs or gun," said the detective.

"Then, you can't say yes, his prints were on the drugs or gun either, correct?"

"No, we can't."

"As a matter of fact, the only reason you are claiming the drugs to be his is because they were found in his car, correct?"

"Yes, that's correct. He's the presumed owner of the drugs and money because he was the owner of the car in which they were found."

"But that disregards all of the other evidence that never even identifies my client as a subject of your undercover investigation, doesn't it detective?"

"Not exactly. Just because he wasn't identified as a subject of our investigation doesn't mean he's not a drug dealer who stored drugs in the glove box of his car."

"But, given the fact that there were others in that house who were found with drugs on their person, who had criminal drug convictions on their records, and the fact that vehicle was easily accessible because it was a soft top, isn't it possible that those drugs could have been placed there by any one of those people in that house?"

"Of course. It's possible," replied the detective.

"How about the gun? Where did you find the gun?" asked Mark.

"The gun was in the closet of an upstairs bedroom where the defendant's duffle bag was found."

"So, how did you decide that the gun was the defendant's?"

"The defendant was living in the room where we found his bag," said the detective.

"Just because you found his bag in the same room where you found a gun in the closet doesn't mean it's his gun, does it?"

"No. But it's reasonable to assume such given the entire totality of the evidence found and collected at the scene," replied the detective.

"Things that are stored in closets of houses, typically belong to people who live there, correct?"

"Typically, yes," the detective replied.

"My client doesn't live in that house and that has been established," said Mark. "Neither the gun nor those drugs belonged to my client. Any number of people who lived in that house could have placed those drugs in my client's car and could have owned that gun."

Mark paused. "I have no further questions your honor," he said as he proceeded back to the defense table.

The prosecution was reeling. Mark had obliterated the testimony of their star witness. They wanted a re-direct cross-examination in an attempt to remedy the damaging effects of Mark's questioning. However, the judge decided to adjourn for the day.

I felt great. My attorney was fighting for me and I believed that any reasonable person would see that I was innocent. The prosecution's entire case was circumstantial at best. They had no evidence that tied me to the drugs found in my car that spring afternoon four months earlier. Things were looking good. But I still didn't want to get too confident. This trial was far from over.

I was escorted back to my jail cell and I took the opportunity to get on my knees and pray. I knew that I needed God's protection every step of the way. My relationship with Him was the calm in the midst of my storm. The next day would be a tough one in court and Mark and I knew it. The prosecutor was going to come out swinging.

The Next Day

I entered the courtroom the next morning feeling a little better than I had the day before. After brief instructions the judge asked, "Does the prosecution want to re-direct cross-examination?"

"Yes, your honor," Mr. Bower stated.

Mr. Bower was looking to undo some of the damage done to the prosecution the day before. He was trying to rebut any assertions by the defense that the investigation was haphazard and that the prosecution's case was more than circumstantial.

Mr. Frampton was called back to the stand and asked a series of questions aimed at discrediting the defense. After excusing Frampton, the prosecution called several other witnesses ranging from the police officers on the scene to forensic officers who handled the evidence. The entire day was a series of direct examination by the prosecution, cross-examination by the defense, and re-direct examination by the prosecution.

I felt like Mark and I had improved our position from the day before. The day was moving along quickly and we had reached the midway point of the afternoon session. The judge called a 15-minute recess, and when the judge sat down to reconvene the session, the prosecutor stood. "May counsel approach the bench, your honor?"

The judge stated that counsel could approach, and I watched as my attorney followed the prosecutor to the front of the courtroom. I had no idea what was being discussed and I sat there with a great deal of apprehension. Finally, the attorneys made their way back to their respective tables as the judge said, "I ask that the jury be removed from the courtroom."

I wondered what was going on as. The jury filed out as instructed, and then the judge spoke. "For the record," he began, "The prosecution believes that the defendant's past criminal conviction should be allowed into evidence given the fact that it shows motive and intent that is relevant to the case at hand."

Mark quickly said, "I disagree with the prosecution, your honor. I believe it would prejudice the jury in the current case, rendering my client unable to obtain a fair trial." The judge listened to both sides of the argument and stated that he would have a decision before the session started the following day.

That decision could turn out to be the game changer for the prosecution… and for me. If the jury found out that six months earlier I had plead guilty to a drug felony, my life was over. There was no way they would be able to judge my guilt or innocence on the merit of the evidence in this case alone. The prosecution knew what it was doing. They were grasping at straws.

The session closed late that afternoon. Before I was taken back to my cell, Mark took me aside. "Frank," he said, "I didn't tell you this before because I didn't think it would come into play. I wanted to put you on the stand because there is no witness who could prove your innocence better than you. However, with your prior felony conviction, it would also give the prosecution the opportunity to bring your conviction into evidence. And that's too risky. Now we may not have a choice in the matter. If the judge allows it, you will have to take the stand in your own defense. It wouldn't necessarily be the end of the world, but it would definitely make it harder for you to walk out of here a free man."

As I was whisked back to jail, my future was hanging in the balance. Just like I had every evening before, I went to God with it. I had nothing else. I prayed and wept, wept and prayed. That night, I slept more peacefully than I had since my arrest.

The Decision

Thursday morning came, the fourth day of the trial, and the only thing on my mind was the judge's decision. I tensed up as I drew closer to the courtroom. When I sat down at the defense table, Mark gripped my shoulder with his hand. "Whatever happens Frank, we're prepared," he said. I tried to smile.

The jury was nowhere in sight. The judge wanted to give his ruling before the jury was present. He entered the courtroom and then sat. "I've made a decision regarding the admissibility of the defendant's prior conviction," he said. "Based upon the law and my interpretation, allowing the defendant's prior conviction into evidence would have a prejudicial impact on the defendant's ability to receive a fair trial. Therefore, I will allow the conviction into evidence only if the defendant takes the stand in his own defense. If not, there will be no admission of it into evidence."

I felt as if I was going to slide off of my chair onto the floor. I was numb. We had dodged the biggest bullet of all. Mr. Bowers recovered, called a few more witnesses, and rested his case. By the afternoon, Mark was presenting my defense.

We only had a few witnesses, a far cry from the large number the prosecution had run through the courtroom—the result of the burden of proof in a criminal case being on the prosecution. The most notable defense witness was my dad who would vouch as to my intentions in Des Moines.

The fourth day of the trial came to a close in the middle of the defense's presentation. We had pretty much seen the worst of what the prosecution had. Their evidence was all on the table. We knew everything we were up against. We planned to finish strong the following day.

I thanked Mark before the guard took me back to my cell. I couldn't believe we were almost finished. My fate was soon to be decided. As I arrived back in my cell, I fell to my knees again in prayer. I was so thankful for the favorable ruling. I was so thankful that God had kept me sane through this entire process. I prayed that His hand would be on me as both sides were slated to rest their cases the following day. Closing arguments would follow. Then, my fate would be in the hands of the jury.

That night, as I lay in my bunk on the sixth floor of the Polk County Jail, I reflected on my life. Freedom or no freedom, my family was dysfunctional. I was dysfunctional, too, but I wanted to be more. There was a good man inside of me. I just needed help to bring him out. I had no mother. I had no father. All I had was God. I wondered where He had been all those years I'd suffered, when it felt like my little brother and I had no protection. Given the pain and darkness I had lived through, I was shocked that I hadn't wound up in jail earlier. Maybe God was the reason I hadn't. Maybe He had a plan for me. But if this were part of it, I wouldn't have wished it on my worst enemy.

God knew my heart, and that night as I lay in my bunk, I made a decision. All of the pain that led me to that day was going to make me a better man, no matter where I spent the next 60 years. God was my Father now and it was Him I would serve, free or behind bars.

When I awoke the next morning, I was ready. I was still terrified because I didn't want to go to prison, but I knew God had more in store for my life.

Arriving at court, the first person I saw was my mother. I had mixed emotions. I was angry with her for letting me take the blame for her crime. But part of me didn't know how to stop loving her.

I sat in my chair, ready for this whole ordeal to be over. Emotionally, I was beat. The proceedings began and I watched in silence as the trial went into early afternoon. Finally, the final witnesses were examined and cross-examined and both the defense and prosecution had rested their cases. Closing arguments were like the final salvo of a Fourth of July fireworks show. It was in the middle of the afternoon on Friday when the judge gave final instructions to the jury and sent them off to deliberate. My life was now in the hands of the jury. Given it was late on Friday, the assumption was that we probably wouldn't get a verdict until the following week.

CHAPTER 12

THE VERDICT

My walk back to the jail that Friday afternoon was filled with anxiety. I wondered how my life had gotten so far off track. I was on the verge of losing my freedom. My life had been reduced to one decision. A verdict.

I entered my cell to begin the awful process of waiting for Monday to learn my fate. I fell to my knees on the cold hard jail floor and prayed with an intensity I had never known before. As my possible destiny flashed in my mind, the desperation of my prayer intensified. There was nothing I could do except plead with the Lord for deliverance. I had read the verse in the Bible that says, "…and the truth will set you free." I was holding steadfast to those words. My hope was rooted in the truth. However, it was out of my hands. I could have had the strength and courage of a thousand men and I still couldn't save myself. Only God could save me now.

I had been on my knees, leaning onto my bunk, for over an hour when the crackling sound of static interrupted my praying. The guard's voice: "Thomas! You're going to court." My stomach turned nauseous with anxiety. This can't be, I thought. It's been less than two hours since deliberations began. I began to panic. The words, "Guilty! Guilty! Guilty!" overpowered my thoughts.

I stood as fear enveloped my body. The door to my cell slowly slid open and locked into position with a clang. There to meet me was a huge guard. He shoved me against the wall, handcuffed me, then lead me to the elevators. "Get in!" I entered the dimly lit elevator and turned around. The elevator doors slammed closed, symbolizing my fate. I felt trapped. My breathing was heavy. There was no turning back.

When the six-floor descent ended, the cold steel doors opened. Two armed guards were there to meet me. They led me to a holding cell where I was re-leased from my handcuffs.

"Put those on," the guard ordered. "Those" consisted of a pair of black pants, a white button-down shirt and a tie. I dressed myself absently. I could have just as easily been a frat boy heading to his homecoming social. But there was every possibility that my party would be a lot more somber.

I finished dressing and sat on the edge of the bunk. I buried my face in my hands and began to cry. "Please Lord, let the jurors have seen the truth," I sobbed. My plea to God was interrupted by footsteps. The guard had come to take me to court. "Step out," he said. "Turn around and put your hands on the wall." I was not one of those defiant, hard-to-handle inmates who hated the guards. I was not a hardheaded or hardhearted kid. I never had a problem with authority figures. So, I did exactly as I was told. I stood facing the wall while I was patted down and searched. Then I was cuffed and shackled.

"Okay, let's go," said the guard. He grabbed me by the arm and led me through the underground corridor that connected the jail and the courthouse. The clanging sound of the chain on my leg shackles reverberated through the dimly lit corridor. So I wouldn't trip and fall, I took short steps that made the 200-yard walk seem as if it would never end. We came to the end and entered the elevator that took us to the third floor of the courthouse.

As we exited, the first person I saw standing outside the courtroom was my father. He appeared much more solemn than the first several days of the trial. I passed right by him without a word.

As I entered the courtroom I saw my mother. Our eyes connected. She stared at me with a look of concern and whispered lowly, "Don't worry. Every-thing is going to be okay." This only made me angry. All I could think was, Sure, everything is going to be okay for you. She wasn't the one locked up, fac-ing sixty years in prison. I was.

I was un-cuffed and led to the defense table. When I took my seat, Mark began to explain to me what was about to happen. But I was in a state of shock, barely processing what he said. His final words to me were low and forebod-ing: "If we don't receive a favorable verdict, we're in a good position for an ap-peal." We were already planning for what would happen after I was found guilty! My immediate thought was, "I'm finished."

Then we were asked to stand, and the jury filed back into the courtroom. I desperately tried to make eye contact with any of them. I wanted to read their eyes. But not one of the twelve jurors would even look at me. Finally, after the last one was seated, the judge entered the courtroom.

After we were all seated, the judge turned his attention to the jury and asked, "Has the jury reached a verdict?" The jury foreman stood. "Yes, we have your honor." My heart was pounding so hard that I felt faint; it was like I had been thrown from an airplane without a parachute.

"Please, receive the verdict," the judge ordered the bailiff.

The bailiff walked a few short paces and received a white, folded sheet of paper from the jury foreman. I stared at it; my life had been reduced to the words on a single sheet of paper. The bailiff handed it to the judge, who opened it and read the verdict to himself. When he was finished his head and eyes rose and all of the attention that was placed on that folded sheet of paper shifted to me. He looked directly into my eyes and asked, "Will the defendant please rise?"

Using the table to steady me, I got to my feet. Mark stood next to me. I felt the weight of everyone's eyes on me. But, otherwise, I was numb.

Without emotion, the judge read the verdict: "We the jury, in the case of the State of Iowa versus Frank Eugene Thomas, Jr., on count one, possession of a controlled substance with the intent to deliver, find the defendant, not guilty. On count two, possession of a controlled substance without possessing the proper drug tax stamp, find the defendant, not guilty. On count three, possession of an illegal firearm, find the defendant, not guilty."

My legs buckled beneath me. Over and over I said, "Thank you Jesus! Thank you Jesus!" I was overwhelmed. All I could think was, Lord, your word is true. The truth will set you free. I could hardly contain myself.

The judge called the court to order, thanked the jurors for their service, and excused them. As the jurors left the jury box and began to exit the courtroom, they passed by the table where I was sitting. When each one approached, with tears in my eyes, I said, "Thank you. Thank you for seeing the truth." One of the jurors, an older Caucasian woman stopped, looked at me and smiled. "We knew you were innocent the entire time," she said. They passed by my mother, who was sitting in the section of the courtroom reserved for public observers. She thanked each of them. It was the greatest victory I have ever experienced. I was free!

The stir in the courtroom calmed down. I was ready to go home. The judge called the court back to order. I thought everything was over. But, to my horror, the judge remanded me back to the custody of the Polk County Jail. Because I was on probation for pleading guilty to a drug offense six months earlier, my probation was in jeopardy despite my acquittal. A probation hearing was set for the next week to determine the possible consequences.

It was like someone had thrown cold water in my face. The euphoria of victory vanished. "Why do I have to go back to jail?" I asked Mark. "I'm innocent!"

He sat me down and explained calmly. "Frank, being arrested, without regard to guilt or innocence, is a violation of your probation," Mark said. "The hearing has been set to determine if your probation is going to be revoked and whether you will be sent to the state penitentiary."

"The state penitentiary? I'm innocent!" This was a nightmare. In seconds, my mood had gone from total, abject relief to fear, apprehension and desperation. I couldn't imagine many fates more cruel.

Cruel Reversal

I was handcuffed and taken back to the county jail. As I entered the sixth floor tier where I was housed, the other inmates were eager to know the verdict of my case. My face must have had a look of grief because as I entered the dayroom one of the inmates shouted, "They got him! I knew it! I saw you on the news, nigga! They weren't going to let you just waltz up outta here!"

"I was found not guilty," I said. "But I have a probation revocation hearing next Tuesday."

"You beat that case?" the inmate asked, incredulously. I nodded. The other prisoners started to clap and shout. My victory was their victory too, a win over The Man. But I couldn't believe I was still in jail and, potentially, facing time in prison.

I spent the weekend in prayer and began to feel somewhat better about the outlook for my future. When the probation hearing came, I arrived in court cuffed and shackled and led by the deputy jailer to the defense table where

Mark was seated. We exchanged pleasantries, but his demeanor was serious.

"Frank," he said, "the prosecutor is recommending to the judge that your probation be revoked and you be sentenced to the maximum term of ten years in prison."

I gawked in shock. "Prison! I'm not going to make it in prison! I was found not guilty! I did everything I was supposed to do according to my probation! Everything!" So I thought.

Mark was unmoved. "You came back to Iowa without notifying your probation officer. Then, when you were subsequently arrested, you also failed to notify them within the required 48 hours," he stated calmly.

"But, I filled out my paperwork every month just like they asked me too. I didn't know I had to notify them that I was going out of town or after I was arrested. I didn't know! If I had known, I would have done the right thing. I didn't know! I didn't even have an actual probation officer in California. If I had known that was a requirement, I wouldn't even have known who to contact!" I pled.

"Frank, I understand. However, when you accepted the plea deal to receive probation that was what you agreed to. You can't assert that you didn't know. It's not going to fly. They're not going to accept that as a valid defense."

I sat in the courtroom dumbfounded and fearful. Even to me, what was going on was clear. The district attorney hadn't been happy about the outcome of my trial. He thought I was guilty and was going to make me pay in some way for beating him. I thought that by the end of the proceeding, I would be going home. Now, it looked like I was on my way to prison.

"However, the district attorney is willing to recommend a 90-day term. With the time you have already served, he's willing to cut it in half to 45 days. If you complete the 45 days with no issues, you'll be placed back on probation. But you're going to have to give up your deferred judgment," Mark continued.

That may have been the biggest blow. With that deferred judgment, as long as I completed my probation, my felony conviction would be expunged from my record. Without it, I would be forever marked as a felon. My life would be ruined.

"Mark, I can't give up the deferred judgment!" I plead. "I'm innocent! I didn't do anything wrong! You don't understand! If I give up that deferred judgment, my life is over. I'll always be a felon. I'll never be able to find a job. I'll never be able to accomplish anything! I can't!" I begged Mark not to let them do this.

"Frank, you don't have a choice. It's either that, or take your chances with the judge. And as your attorney, I strongly advise you to take the prosecutor's deal. Otherwise, you will most likely have your probation violated, your deferred judgment taken away, and you will be sentenced to ten years in prison with no guarantee of a release date. By taking this deal, yes, they'll send you to prison for forty-five days but you'll be released back out on probation. This is as good as it gets."

I knew I didn't have a choice. I couldn't live up to my potential in prison. I needed my freedom. I reluctantly told Mark that I would take the deal. But I would be a convicted felon for the rest of my life. I thought that, at 20 years old, my life was over.

The judge called the hearing to order. The prosecutor brought forth a motion to revoke my probation and entered his recommendation. Then the judge called on my attorney: did he agree that my original suspended sentence of ten years in prison be reinstated and deferred judgment forfeited? He did.

For the second time in less than a week, the judge asked me to rise. I stood to hear his ruling. "Does the defendant understand the motion and recommendation for sentencing?" the judge asked me.

"I do, your honor," I replied.

"I hereby impose the sentence that the probation for Frank E. Thomas, Jr. be revoked and that his ten-year suspended sentence be imposed. I hereby order that his deferred judgment be revoked and he be remanded to Iowa State Department of Corrections."

Just like that, I was headed to prison.

#1010486

In short order, I was loaded into a special van along with several other prisoners headed to the Iowa Medical and Classification Center (IMCC) in Oakdale, Iowa—the state's maximum security prison and point of reception for all prisoners who are sentenced to serve prison time in Iowa.

The journey took about two hours. Once we arrived, the other inmates and I were shackled together just like a chain gang out of an old prison movie. I was walked past what seemed like miles of tall fencing topped with razor wire. To say I was afraid was an understatement. I was nearly frozen with terror. I was really in prison.

Inside the walls of the massive building were some of the most violent men the state of Iowa had ever seen. They'd been convicted of murder, rape, pedophilia, you name it. "I don't belong here," was all I could think. However, the truth was that I had broken the law and compromised my personal values. This was where they took people who did such things. But I knew that I wasn't a criminal. I was a kid who had made some bad choices. Now, I would pay dearly for those mistakes.

Chained together, the other inmates and I made our way into the building. We were strip searched and then taken into a room to await our individual intakes. I was subjected to a barrage of questions surrounding my health, drug use, education, gang affiliations, etc. I was told the rules of prison and ordered to sign a written acknowledgment pledging that I would abide by all of them. Then I was given my number. From that point forward, I would be known as inmate #1010486. My life no longer belonged to me. I was a piece of property that belonged to the state of Iowa.

After the intake process, we were taken to another room and issued our standard issue prison garb: dingy, stained underwear, a t-shirt and socks. Our outerwear was a beige medical scrub suit that you might find nurses or doctors wearing at your local hospital. But on the back in bold black letters it read, "Iowa Department of Corrections".

Finally, it was time to matriculate into the general prison population. As the guard led me to the unit I was assigned to, my anxiety was so extreme I was practically levitating. I heard about prison life: the homosexuality, rapes, and rampant violence. As the door to the unit opened and I was led through, the inmates clapped and whistled. Apparently this was a normal prison hazing ritual for new arrivals. I was scared out of my mind, but did everything I could to hide it. I did not want to show any weakness for fear that someone would try to prey on me.

Then I was shocked to see a familiar face: my older cousin Aaron. Like me, he was there on a drug conviction. While it's the last place I would want to see someone I love, under the circumstances, I was relieved to know that I wasn't going to have to go through this on my own. When I saw Aaron I knew that everything was going to be okay. I knew he would have my back and I would have his.

My assigned cell was cold and eerie, with nothing but a bed, stainless steel toilet and sink. My bunk was anchored to the wall with a bright orange mattress pad that couldn't have been more than two or three inches thick. This would be my home for the next 45 days—or at least until a bed opened up at another prison that fit my low-risk classification.

So I settled in for my brief but all-too-lengthy stay in prison. Each day I would rise and check off another day in my running countdown of the 45 days I had to serve. But in the back of my mind, I was fearful that the 45 day agreement was not going to be honored. After all, it had not been stated anywhere on my paperwork. I prayed that the judge would keep his word. I was in prison and I had little to no communication with the outside world.

While I sat in my cell each day, I had plenty of time to think about my future. I knew God have given me another chance with my acquittal on the drug charges. I promised Him that I would take full advantage of it. I knew I had to be a man of action. Each day, I sat in my cell thinking that from this point on, I would do everything I knew I needed to do without hesitating or making excuses. I wasn't going to act based on how I felt but on what I knew was best. When I lay down to go to sleep and remembered that I had forgotten to say my prayers, I would jump up and pray without regard to how tired I was. I couldn't afford to allow myself to be complacent about the life that God had given me. I had to be on a mission to improve my life and myself. I made a pact with myself and with God that I was going to be as focused as a man could possibly be.

Minimum Security

On September 30, 1991—Day 42 of my prison incarceration—I was told to pack my things. I could only assume I was being moved to another unit. However, I was taken to a room where I was processed out of the facility. I was cuffed and shackled and loaded into a van and given no information. The van drove off and I stared out the window at the fortress-like prison. "I'll never return to this place again," I thought. Then I settled in for the ride.

An hour later, the van pulled up to a small facility that resembled a farm. There were neither fences nor barbed wire. There were men walking around in blue jeans and shirts that read, "Iowa Department of Corrections." There was a sign that said, "Newton Correctional Facility." Newton Correctional Facility was in a small town about thirty-five miles east of Des Moines. Newton was a minimum-security prison for inmates who pose a very low risk to society. This was my final stop before freedom.

I had three days remaining before my release. Because I was now in a facility outside of the central processing center, I could have visitors. On my forty-fourth day of incarceration, I got a visit from Ali. She had stayed by my side through the entire ordeal. It was the first time that I'd had the opportunity to hug anyone who loved me since June 3, 1991, the day I turned myself in—a total of 122 days. It felt like a lifetime. So much had transpired during that period. That day we shed tears of pain and joy because we recognized how close we had come to never seeing one another again. One more day and we could put this nightmare behind us.

CHAPTER 13

GOING BACK TO CALI

On the morning of October 3, 1991, one of the guards ordered me to gather my belongings. I packed as quickly as I could. I was loaded into a van and driven thirty-five minutes to Des Moines and the Polk County Jail. At the jail I was able to change into the clothes that I had been wearing when I had turned myself in more than four months earlier. I signed some paperwork and I was free to go.

I was walked through a series of heavy-duty security doors. When the final door opened and I stepped through, tears began rolling down my face. I was finally free. For twenty years I had endured poverty, pain, and hopelessness, but I knew that my life had been transformed. I stepped into that jail a broken, scared little boy but I was leaving a man on a mission. I promised God and myself that I would let nothing keep me from achieving the success I knew I was capable of. I had no idea what was in front of me. I was a convicted felon with every excuse to roll over and die. But I wouldn't. The spirit inside of me said, "Rise and fight." I had gotten a dose of perspective—a new life. I was so grateful and determined to live that I vowed, "Even death can't stop me!"

It was a cold, rainy fall day in Des Moines. I had no money. No one knew that I had been released. I stood on the corner for several minutes, trying to collect myself. Finally, I crossed the street to a payphone and placed a collect call to my mother's house. "Hello," Ali answered. "Would you accept a collect call from Frank Thomas?" the operator asked.

"Yes!" she replied excitedly. "Frank? Hello?" she asked.

"Hello. Babe, it's me. I'm free!" I shouted.

"Where are you?"

"In front of the Polk County Jail."

"I'm on my way. I love you!" she said.

"I love you too!" I said as I hung up the phone.

Without Ali, I'm not sure that I would have made it. When she pulled up to that corner that day, I jumped into the car and we embraced. I thanked her again and again for not giving up on me or losing hope. Beyond my newfound faith in God, our relationship was the only thing I had that made any sense. I could trust her love. She had always been there for me.

Then we drove to my mother's house, where Ali had been living during my incarceration. So began the emotional roller coaster ride. In seconds, I went from joy to fear and anger. I loved my mother; she was the only parent I had ever really had. But how could she have allowed me to be her sacrificial lamb—to go down for her crime?

For all my worry, my mother couldn't see straight. She was so far under the influence of drugs, alcohol and money that I didn't even know her anymore. She had moved out of my grandmother's house shortly after the raid because my grandmother would no longer allow drug dealing in her house. Also, her house was "hot" now, meaning that because it was a location where known illegal drug trafficking had occurred, the cops would be watching it constantly.

Because of the risk my mother posed, I wasn't excited about the prospect of staying at her house after my release. I didn't trust her. Making it worse was the fact that she never even apologized for what she had done to me. But I had no other options. I had no money, no car, and no job. I needed her and a place to live until I could meet with my probation officer and get their consent to move back to California.

When Ali and I arrived at my mother's house nobody was home, but my mother showed up not long after we got there. She greeted me with a hug and welcomed me home. There was awkwardness, at least from my perspective. However, she acted as if nothing had happened. My mother had always been tough and hard. But, becoming a drug dealer had taken her to another level. She was always high and always drinking. I didn't even recognize her because she had become so callous and medicated. It finally hit me: she was a gangster.

Nothing was going to keep her from making money.

Giving Into My Mother

The three of us sat in her kitchen talking for a while. Ali got up and went into the bedroom to take a nap, and my mother and I were alone. Suddenly, she reached out to hand me a small sandwich bag and asked, "Will you cook this for me?" I stood there, frozen. It was cocaine.

Cooking cocaine in hot water and baking soda was how drug dealers turned powder cocaine into crack. I rue the day I ever learned the first thing about drugs, let alone learning how to "rock up" powder cocaine. I looked at her in shock.

"Oh! Don't worry! Ain't nothing going to happen!" she said in a harsh tone. She wasn't asking me. She was "suggesting" that I do what she asked just like she always did. I was stunned. After all I'd been through, how could she even propose such a thing? Just the sight of the drugs turned my stomach. All I could think was, "What if the police raid this place?" My mother just stood there expecting me take the bag and do as she wished. After several tense, awkward seconds, I opened my hand and she dropped the bag into my palm. Once again, I didn't have the courage to stand up to her.

While I cooked that cocaine, I was shaking and sweating so much that I thought I would pass out. Even before it was finished hardening into its rock form, I threw down the spoon that I was using, grabbed a sweatshirt and made my way to the door.

"Where you going?" she asked.

"For a walk!" I replied. I opened the door and stepped out into a driving rainstorm. I slammed the door behind me and began to walk. My mother was sick in the head. She didn't care about me. She didn't even care about herself. She didn't care about anybody or anything except getting high, getting drunk and making money. She didn't care that she almost cost me 60 years of my life. She had no remorse.

I walked and walked and walked, praying, tearfully every step of the way. I was soaked and freezing. But the last thing that I wanted to do was go back to my mother's house. So I just kept walking. Suddenly, a blue Lincoln Town Car pulled up next to me. It was my oldest cousin Jamal. He rolled down his window and shouted, "What's up cuzz? You okay?"

Choking on my tears, I coughed out, "Yeah, I'm okay!" His car continued at a crawl next to me as I kept walking.

"Get in man, it's wet and cold out there."

"No!"

"What's wrong man?"

"Leave me alone! I'm okay!"

"Okay," he said and drove off.

I had made a promise to God that I would never touch drugs again and I hadn't been out of prison for more than a few hours and I had already broken that promise. I was disgusted with myself and felt like I was never going to be able to escape my brokenness. I wanted to get far away from my family and from Des Moines. I couldn't help but think back to January 1990 and the time my mother and I came through Des Moines on the way to the University of Wyoming. I knew then that the city was a cesspool where blacks came to rot and die. I wanted nothing to do with it. Now, it had chewed me up and spit me out. I felt like my life was nothing more than wreckage.

What was I going to do now?

Probation Again

As part of the condition of my release, I was expected to check in with the office of the Department of Probation within 48 hours. The day after my cold, despairing, soggy walk, I called the office and set up an appointment to meet my supervising probation officer. This time, I would make sure that I understood every condition of my probation. I could not take the chance that I might violate it due to a misunderstanding.

My appointment was with Lynelle Hawthorne, the same probation officer I'd had after my first arrest. I showed up to my appointment early, nervous because I didn't want anything to jeopardize the transfer of my probation to California. My life was in California. I needed to get away from the alcoholism, drug dealing and darkness that had gripped almost every member of my family.

I sat quietly in the waiting area. Finally, Ms. Hawthorne appeared and said, "Frank." We walked down a narrow hallway and she stopped near the restroom and handed me a small cup with a lid on it. I knew exactly what it was. She looked at me and said, "You know the drill." I did. A male probation officer followed me into the bathroom to ensure my specimen was legit. I peed in the cup, fastened the lid tightly, and put it in the officer's rubber-gloved hand.

This was protocol. If your urine was "dirty," probation could be violated immediately. If that happened, you were arrested on the spot and taken to jail to await your day in court. This was not a situation anyone wanted to find themselves in. I wasn't worried, though. I had never ingested a drug in my life and I hadn't had any alcohol in over four months. Finally, I took a seat in Ms. Hawthorne's office.

"Frank, you're one lucky man," she said. "I don't know how you beat that case. I didn't think I would see you back here."

"I was innocent, Ms. Hawthorne," I said. "I didn't do anything wrong. They arrested and tried the wrong person. I'm not a troublemaker. But I made a mistake and now, I'll have to live with the consequences for the rest of my life. But you don't ever have to worry about seeing me in trouble again. I promise you that."

In a voice that made me believe she had heard this song and dance before, she said, "I hope you're right, Frank." She flipped some papers. "Now, are you trying to transfer your probation back to California?" she asked.

"Yes, please. I have to get out of here," I responded.

"That shouldn't be a problem."

"Thank you Jesus!" I said under my breath.

She proceeded to ask me a series of questions. In the middle of the process, the officer who had taken my urine sample walked into the office.

"His urine is clean."

I sighed with relief. It was one less hurdle on my road to redemption. I had learned through this ordeal that being innocent doesn't mean you won't be charged and potentially even found guilty. The only way to keep from being unnecessarily exposed to trouble is not to allow yourself to be around people or situations where you can be compromised—even if it means you have to turn and walk away from your entire family.

That's why I knew I needed to get out of Des Moines. My fear wasn't about what I would do. My fear was that if I couldn't get out, the constant exposure to addiction, crime and hopelessness would not only endanger my freedom but my very soul. If you are who you spend your time with, then I was tired of being a man who spent his time with lost and broken souls.

Ms. Hawthorne went on to explain the terms of my probation. This time, I asked plenty of questions. I was not leaving until I knew exactly what my responsibilities were. As we wrapped up the meeting, she looked at me intently. "Do you have any final questions?"

I looked her in the eyes and said, "No. I get it this time."

"Great, Frank," she replied. "Travel safely back to California. I wish you luck, and I hope I never see you again under these circumstances."

I left her office happy and scared—happy because I was free, but scared for the exact the same reason. I didn't want to disappoint her. I didn't want to disappoint Judge Hutchison. I didn't want to disappoint Mark, my attorney. I didn't want to disappoint Ali. I didn't want to disappoint myself. And, most importantly, I didn't want to disappoint God, whose grace and mercy had set me free.

I had my probation transfer papers in hand and was ready to make my way back to Southern California—the place where, just nine months earlier, I'd landed for the first time. I still felt sure that it was where all of my dreams would come true. The time had come to journey home. But first, I went back to my mother's house one last time to let everyone know I was leaving.

Westward

When I got to the house, everyone was sitting in the living room, talking. I walked in and Ali jumped up when she saw me. "Is everything okay? Can you go back to California?" she asked nervously.

"Yes! It's time for us to get on the road," I said to her as we hugged. I didn't want to waste a second. Time was of the essence. I feared the dark gravitational pull of that place. Every second we stayed in Des Moines, it felt like something terrible could happen.

So Ali and I packed up her silver Geo Spectrum. When we finished, the car was loaded from floor to roof with a small space cleared for seeing through the rearview mirror. Finally, we said our goodbyes and drove away. I felt a peace overcome me. I felt like I was starting over. The 27-hour journey between Des Moines and San Diego was like being reborn. Des Moines had been my death. San Diego would be my resurrection.

We drove the entire trip non-stop, switching drivers when one of us got tired. I was on a mission. The sooner we got there, the sooner I could exorcise my demons. I was no longer going to depend on anyone else and start crying if things didn't turn out like I wanted them to. I had a vision and dreams and I was willing to pay whatever price was required to see them come to pass.

When we arrived in San Diego, we drove up to the small house where Ali and I had lived together with her sister and her sister's boyfriend. It was a sight for sore eyes. When I parked the car, I breathed a sigh of relief. Yes, I was exhausted from the twenty-seven hour journey. But I was just so thankful to be back. The past year had been hell. I felt like now, I could rest easy and let my guard down.

Ali rang the doorbell. Her sister and her sister's boyfriend answered and welcomed us in. We exchanged hugs, sat down to talk for a few minutes, and then began to unload the car. I was overwhelmed with humility. I was a free man in San Diego—the most beautiful city in the world—with the person I loved most. Overcome with God's goodness, I slept like a baby that first night home.

CHAPTER 14

CONVICTED FELON

PART 1

Shortly after our arrival, a harsh reality set it. The country was still in the middle of a severe economic recession and companies were slashing payrolls. It wasn't exactly an ideal time for twenty-year-old kid with a high school education and a felony conviction to find a job. With a felony on my record, I felt like Hester Prynne from The Scarlet Letter. There was nowhere for me to hide.

Still, I had no choice. I had to find a job. I'd made a promise to God that He would never have to worry about me messing up. It was His grace that delivered me from my lion's den. I knew that He didn't bring me all this way to die a pauper. I believed that if I remained determined, He would help me find a job. So I began the process of seeking employment.

The good news was that I had a lot of work experience. I'd worked for almost seven years in various warehouse and retail sales positions in my uncle's business in Kansas City. I'd worked as a busboy at the Marriott hotel. I'd even worked as a janitor, cleaning movie theatres after hours for my Uncle Lawrence's neighbor. The summer I lived in Denver, I worked as a bagger at King Sooper's grocery store. The greatest asset I had to offer any company was my unrelenting work ethic. I never claimed to be the smartest guy in the world, but I didn't know anyone who could outwork me.

But after a month of searching with no luck, I began to panic. Each morning I would scour the classified ads. I made phone calls and walked around filling out applications but got no interviews. It had to be that dreaded question, "Have you ever been convicted of a felony?" The second I answered that question in the affirmative, any chance of landing an interview was gone. I was becoming discouraged and desperate.

I had no idea how I was going to get a job if everyone turned me down. I'd made some awful choices and learned some hard lessons. But I didn't think it should be held against me for the rest of my life! Like it nor not, I still had to make a living. I couldn't just quit. So I kept pounding the pavement, looking in the classifieds, and filling out applications. Something was going to have to give at some point.

Then one day, while I was going through the classifieds, I noticed a listing from an employment agency that helped jobseekers find work. Figuring I had nothing to lose, I called the number. When the receptionist answered I mentioned to her that I saw their ad in the newspaper and that I was interested in speaking with someone about it. She put me through to a man who began to ask me several questions. He asked me what level of education I had and what type of work experience. I shared with him what I had done in the past and that I only had a high school diploma. "Could you come to our offices tomorrow for an interview?" he asked.

"Sure! What time and where?"

He gave me the address and the time and I thanked him. It looked like something was finally coming through.

That morning, I got dressed in the best clothes I owned—khaki pants, a button-down shirt and a simple necktie. I didn't have the money to buy a suit. I dropped Ali off at work and used her car to attend the interview.

The office building was in the historic Old Town section of San Diego and looked pretty beat up. It didn't look or feel like a professional company would have offices there. I was a little skeptical as I made my way up the elevator to the third floor. When I opened the door to the suite, my skepticism deepened: dark brown wood panel walls combined with burnt orange and yellow furniture made the office look like something out of the Brady Bunch.

A receptionist was sitting behind a makeshift desk. "How can I help you?" she asked politely.

"My name is Frank Thomas and I'm here for my ten a.m. interview," I said.

"Please take a seat, he'll be right with you," as she pointed me toward the hideous furniture. I took a seat and waited. I couldn't help but keep glancing at the ugly décor. But that was the least of my concerns. I was just hoping this guy could help me find a job.

After several minutes an older guy with salt-and-pepper colored hair came out.

"Frank?" he said.

"Yes sir," I replied as we shook hands.

"Come back here with me," he replied.

I followed him to an office even more dreadful than the reception area.

After asking me a series of questions, he explained to me how the process would work.

"We require candidates to pay sixty percent of their first month's wages over a three month time frame if we find a position for you," he said. "I have a company in mind where I believe you would be a great fit." I sat there stunned for a second. Sixty percent of my first month's wages? It was highway robbery. But then I heard my grandfather's words: "Some money beats no money." This was true, and considering my circumstances, I really didn't have a choice. While sixty-percent of my first month's wages wasn't ideal, if he could help me get a job I was willing to pay the price.

"Okay. Sounds good," I responded.

"Great. Fill these forms out and give them to the receptionist when you're finished. I will be in touch with you in a day or two," he said.

"Thank you so much! I look forward to hearing from you," I said as we shook hands.

The next day, he called to tell me he'd gotten me an interview for a labor position. The company was a small, family-owned manufacturing company in National City, a small suburban city just outside San Diego. I was to show up the next day and ask for the plant manager, Michael McNearney. I hung up the phone ecstatic. I needed this job. I prayed that God would help me close the deal.

The Interview

At the office the next morning, I told the receptionist I was there for an interview with Mr. McNearney. She gave me a pen and a clipboard. "Fill this out and let me know when you are finished," she said. "Then I will page Michael."

On the clipboard was a form with the heading, "EMPLOYMENT APPLI-CATION" in bold letters. I scanned it quickly. About halfway down the page there it was, that dreaded question: "Have you ever been convicted of a felony?" I wondered if I should just forget it and walk away. I cursed my mother. It was her fault that I'd lost my deferred judgment. But this was my reality, and I knew I couldn't run from it forever. I started to fill out the application.

When I got to the felony question, I decided to skip it and come back to it. I completed the remainder of the application. Finally, only that horrible question remained unanswered. Clutching the pen, I tried to check the "YES" box but I couldn't do it. Then, impulsively, I checked the box that said, "NO". I sat there miserably, knowing I'd lied. In order to justify my actions to myself, I made a silent pledge that if they gave me a job, I would be the best damn worker they'd ever seen.

After several minutes I collected myself and returned the employment application to the receptionist. Her eyes scanned every line. It felt almost as if she knew I had lied. Almost worse than telling the employer the truth was the fear of being exposed and humiliated for lying. I hated myself.

The receptionist looked up at me. "Okay. I'll call Michael now," she said. "Please have a seat. He'll be right out."

I swallowed hard. "Okay. Thank you," I said, and sat back down. Within minutes, the plant manager, came in. He was silver-haired and about 60 years old.

"Frank. Mike McNearney. Pleasure to meet you," he said as he reached out to shake my hand. "Follow me."

We made our way through the manufacturing plant. There were men welding and working on heavy machinery. There was a lot of smoke, oil and dirt. Mike took me to his office high above the plant floor. It had glass walls on all four sides, which allowed a 360-degree view of the factory floor below. "Have a seat," he said.

The interview lasted for about forty-five minutes. During the course of the interview, Mike shared with me how he was a retired seaman who served over 20 years in the Navy. That explained his tough, no-nonsense approach. Although he was rough around the edges, I could tell he was a pretty nice guy.

"Do you have any questions, Frank?" Mike asked.

"No. I don't think so. You've done a great job of explaining the position, your company, and its business. Thank you." I said.

"Well, let me take you on a quick tour of the plant," he said.

Mike walked me around every station in the plant and explained each department in detail. When he finished, he asked, "So, when can you start?"

"Immediately," I said.

"How 'bout tomorrow?"

"I'll be here," I said. "Oh. But, what's the pay rate?"

Mike laughed. "Oh yeah. It's six dollars per hour," he said.

"Perfect, Mike!" I replied. I'll see you first thing in the morning. Thank you!"

We shook hands and he showed me out.

As I walked to the car, I couldn't even enjoy the fact that I had landed a job because the only thing I could think about was the lie I told on the employment application. It was just a matter of time before it was exposed. My only hope was to work my tail off and show Mike I was the hardest and smartest worker he'd ever hired. Hopefully, by the time my lie was uncovered, he would see my work ethic and look past my mistakes.

Western Lifts, Inc.

On Thursday, November 21, 1991, I started my first day at Western Lifts, Inc. From the day I showed up, I worked harder than I had ever worked in my life. I didn't take one second of downtime while I was on the clock. I was on a quest to show Mike that I was the best hire he'd ever made. And it didn't take long for my work ethic to be put to the test.

Approximately seven weeks after I started, just after the New Year in 1992, I heard through the rumor mill that the company would be going through a round of layoffs. I was sick. All I could think was, "Last one hired, first one fired." The last person hired had been me.

I needed this job. I hadn't even paid the employment agency back yet. How could this be happening? How could you hire someone and lay them off seven weeks later? Couldn't you just look at your projections of future business and know that you didn't need the additional help? These questions and more ran through my head. It just didn't make sense.

About two hours before the end of the shift, Mike began calling people into his office one at a time to give them their walking papers. Surprisingly, I wasn't the first person called. I watched one person after another walk up the staircase to Mike's office. One by one they were sent home. All I knew was that I would continue working my tail off. Who knows what could happen? Maybe business would turn around quickly and I would be one of the first people they hired back.

The shift was nearing its end. When the horn sounded, I shut my machine off, gathered all of my personal items, and made my way to the time clock to punch out. I saw a guy coming down from the office with Mike right behind him. From the look on his face, I could tell he'd just gotten the axe. I figured there was no sense in me prolonging the inevitable, so I walked to the base of the stairs and called up to Mike, "So, do I come back tomorrow?"

Mike descended the staircase, looked at me with an intensity that only a veteran could muster, and growled, "You're damn right you come back tomorrow! You keep doing what you're doing and you'll always have a job here!"

A wave of relief washed over me. "Thank you!" I said.

God knew I needed that job. On the way home, I started to weep tears of gratitude. God was looking out for me. When I made those promises to Him in the Polk County Jail, He knew I was sincere. All I wanted was a second chance. I got one. Now it was up to me to make something of it.

Things were on the uptick for me. I had a good job at a company that valued my contribution. My relationship with Ali was great. We had finally gotten our own apartment. My life was beginning to expand. But while things were going really well for me, back home in Des Moines things were deteriorating.

The Call

My mother had become the female version of Nino Brown from the movie New Jack City. She was going deeper and deeper into drugs and now my brother, Montez, had walked through the door, too. It was only a matter of time before he would be working corners trying to turn a fast buck. Crack cocaine and the allure of the fast money it generated was tearing my family apart and wasn't going to stop until there was no one left.

Many nights I would go to sleep thinking about the safety of my mother and brother. I feared receiving a call in the middle of the night notifying me that one or both of them had been shot and killed, hurt badly, or arrested. It was inevitable. My greatest worry, however, was how I would respond to the news. I was afraid that my grief might cause me to retaliate on their behalf. I was grateful that I was so far away from Des Moines; if something happened to my mother or brother, I would hopefully have time to cool off before I got back with vengeance on my mind.

The call I dreaded came in March of 1992. Montez called to tell me that my mother and father had been arrested after leading police on a high-speed chase after selling drugs to an informant. During the chase they were throwing drugs and money out of the car. The whole thing had even been caught on camera and broadcast on the national news. I sighed. I had known this was coming. I just didn't think it would come so soon—less than six months after I escaped Des Moines. For their crimes, both my mother and father each were sentenced to ten years in the state penitentiary. While I was upset it had come to this, a part of me was relieved that my mother was off the streets. I wouldn't have to worry much about her safety while she was incarcerated. But I still had to worry about my younger brother.

Working Hard

While I continued to watch crack annihilate my family from afar, my life continued to get better. Within six months of being hired at Western Lifts I received my first promotion. I went from making $6 per hour to making $10.50 per hour. My hard work was paying off. I could hardly believe it. My first thought was, "I don't know anybody in my family making double-digit dollars per hour legally." It felt like I had made it. I could finally take care of myself without relying on anyone else.

My second thought was, "I'm going to retire from this company." I always wanted a great paying job and I'd finally gotten it. It wasn't going to be long before I was making fifteen to eighteen dollars per hour like the most senior guys in the plant. That's the kind of pay I was shooting for. Money was always my problem—not having enough of it. This job was helping me solve that problem legally.

I worked hard. I gave everything I had, every day. I tried to learn every job in the plant. Six months after my first promotion, I got huge pay increase. Most employees got a cost-of-living-adjustment, which equated to about three to four percent of their hourly salary. I went from ten dollars and fifty cents per hour to twelve dollars per hour, an increase of more than 14 percent. My work ethic had won me favor with my boss and I had only been at the company for one year. At the rate I was going, I'd be running the plant before long.

With the substantial raises came greater expectations, though. But that was okay. I didn't mind because I loved working hard. I was like the Energizer bunny all day long. The more proficient I became, the less time it took me to do my job. That freed me up to learn the other jobs in the plant and help other departments get things done.

I was motivated by money because of the poverty of my youth. When I had money, I felt secure. When I didn't, I felt worthless and needy. So, whenever the company had overtime—voluntary or involuntary—I was always there. But after a while, my endless hard work got me teased by my coworkers. "Slow down," they'd say, "you're making us look bad."

This made me mad. "I'm not making you look bad," I'd reply. "You're making you look bad. This company pays me to work and that's what I'm going to do." But the teasing only got worse.

Whenever Mike was talking to me, guys would walk by, pucker their lips, make a loud kissing sound and call me "butt-kisser", "brown noser" and worse. When Mike would turn around to look they would turn away and act as if they had said nothing. Some teased me by saying Mike was my daddy. I always caught flak because I chose to excel at what I was doing while most guys wanted to get as much money as they could while doing as little work as possible.

Mike's confidence in my abilities grew and because of that he would lay more expectations on me. Soon, I was the one who was rallying the troops to meet almost impossible deadlines. The guys hated to see me coming. I just wanted to do a great job and would try to inspire them to join in. Most of the time they would. However, it wouldn't be without the teasing and harassment that I had become accustomed to. It really didn't bother me. I knew they were jealous because I had the boss' favor.

The more responsibility I took on, the more Mike expected of me. At times it felt like it was too much to bear. After a while, it I started to feel as though he was taking me for granted. It was as if he had gotten used to me working myself into the ground; what was once superior performance became my new baseline. I had become a victim of my own success. This would continue throughout my second year at the company…and one day, it spilled over.

CHAPTER 15

REVELATION

Mike had become exceedingly dependent on my ability to motivate and inspire the guys to make uncommon things happen at the plant. Regardless of how tall the order, he knew I was up for the challenge and he counted on my leadership to get things done. And despite being constantly teased by the guys at the plant, I had their respect. They knew I was all about business—doing a great job right and as quickly as possible. But in spite of all the raises I'd gotten, there were many times when Mike put too much pressure on me and regarded me as a robot. I began to feel like my work and dedication were unappreciated. This began to take a toll on me.

One day, Mike came down from his office and into my area of the plant. A specific order that was to be shipped to Saudi Arabia wasn't going out on time. I knew the order was behind schedule and it had nothing to do with me. The difference was that this time, I wasn't going out to rally the troops. I decided to stay in my department and do only my job. However, instead of going to the source of the delay, Mike came straight to me. He had gotten so used to me driving the other guys in the plant to get things done that if something wasn't going right he immediately came to me to ask what the problem was. This time things would change forever.

Mike was on the warpath, "Boy, why in the fuck isn't this order going out on time? What the fuck is going on?" He asked.

At that, I snapped. "I've never raised my voice at you!" I shouted back. "I have never called you by anything other than your name! I'm a man before I'm anything! You will not disrespect me!"

I could feel my mouth foaming. Mike immediately backed off. "Okay," he said. "Calm down. Just calm down."

I turned and walked away, and as I did I had a revelation: I had to get out of that plant. Getting a college education was my only ticket out. At the time, Ali was a full-time student attending San Diego State and she became my vision of what was possible. But our relationship had begun to sour because, truth be told, I was envious of her life. She was living a dream Southern California life and her father was supporting it. As long as she was in school, he would make sure she was taken care of. I, on the other hand, was busting my rump without the luxury of any support or a safety net. She was creating the life of her dreams using education as the vehicle and I was simply surviving. I needed a paycheck.

My jealousy of her and her situation led me to focus only on our differences. We were two young people who came from different worlds and had different destinies. I began to tell myself that she didn't really understand my struggle, and unconsciously I began to sabotage our relationship. I didn't know how to deal with and express the depths of the emotions I was feeling so I would either shut down or act out. We eventually agreed it would be best for us to live separately, and before long, I cheated on her again.

When I told her what I'd done, she left me. I didn't blame her. I had betrayed her trust. She was finished. She deserved more than I was capable of giving her. When she was gone, I regretted it. I wanted her back. But she moved on with her life.

My breakup with Ali and my altercation with Mike took away what doubts I had. While I'd thought about going back to school from time-to-time, it was now clear that the only way I was going to move forward in life was to get an education. If I didn't, I would end up just like the forty-year-old guys who worked in the plant—the ones who had been there since they graduated from high school. Sure they were making $20 per hour—which was like a million dollars a year to me. But what would happen if, God forbid, the company went out of business? What would happen to me then? I didn't know too many hydraulic hoist-manufacturing companies in the U.S. The hard skills that I was acquiring were not exactly transferable to another industry.

I suddenly realized that with the wrong breaks, I might find myself working at McDonalds at thirty-five years old. I knew that was not my destiny. I knew I was going to have to go back to college in order to have more options.

Mike and I ended up working things out that day. We apologized to each other. He was surprised at how I responded; he'd thought I was going to be a pushover because he was paying me so well and he had given me favor. If I didn't have his respect before, I had it now. And while I was grateful for all he had done for me, I also worked my tail off. I earned everything I'd gotten and made him look good in the bargain.

That day I learned two valuable lessons. First, always do my best to make my bosses look good and they would take care of me. Secondly, I teach people how to treat me; never let anyone disrespect me simply because of their position of authority. If I didn't stand up for myself they'd believe it was okay to continue to treat me in a disrespectful manner.

Back to School

In January of 1994—shortly after my confrontation with Mike—I found myself at San Diego Mesa Community College, completing an application for admission and registering to take the Math and English placement exams. I was 22 years old. I had been working for Western Lifts just over two years. I knew the time had come for me to start planning for my future instead of just waiting for the future to come to me.

I enrolled in two courses that spring semester—math and political science. I would work all day and when the horn went off at 4:30pm, I would change out of my dirty work clothes and head to campus for a 6:00pm class. I did this twice a week. The days that I didn't have class I would go to the campus library and do homework. During the weekends, I started spending the majority of my time studying. I worked hard at work, but I worked even harder at school.

When that first semester ended I finished with two As. I was proud of myself for making the commitment to school while working full time and earning good grades to boot. I enrolled in one class during the summer session and received another A. Something inside me started to believe, "I can do this."

That same summer I went back to Des Moines to visit my family because my mother had been released from prison after serving almost two years. I hadn't seen her in almost three. After leaving Des Moines the last time I had no desire to return, but I missed my family. I was living in California all by myself and I longed for something familiar.

But when I arrived, I realized that nothing had changed. Drugs, alcohol, and hopelessness were still pervasive. Many of the faces had changed, but for the most part, they were still getting high, getting drunk, and selling drugs. It didn't take long for me to become sick to my stomach all over again. I had left this place for a reason. Why did I ever come back here? I would ask myself that same question at several junctures during my visit. Before it was over, I would experience an episode of ugliness and truth that would shatter me.

Physically, my mother looked great. She had lost weight while in prison. I had missed her tremendously. While she never apologized to me for what had happened with the drugs she placed in my car, I had long since forgiven her. I needed to free myself from the bondage of holding a grudge. I'd even forgiven her for abandoning Montez and me as kids. I'd realized that she had done the best she could with what she was given, and that wasn't much. I'd come to realize that God had allowed the incident with the drugs in my car to happen in order to shake up both of our lives. He wanted to give us a chance to wake up and get right with Him. I took the opportunity and began to try to build a better life. My mother would need many more years and bruises to learn to do the same.

Heartbreak

This was also the first time that I'd seen my brother in well over a year. When my mother was sentenced to prison, he'd come to live with Ali and me in San Diego. I didn't want him falling victim to the lure of fast money the same way our mother and I did. My hope was that he and I could be brothers again, just like we had been growing up. But our relationship had lost its closeness. He didn't last two months in San Diego. I came home from work one day to find out that he had jumped on a Greyhound bus back to Des Moines. I couldn't force him to stay.

Since then, the thing I had feared for him actually happened: he had gotten pulled into the streets. He was dealing drugs and smoking weed. We both knew how messed up our lives were because of our mother's and father's drug and alcohol abuse, and we'd had an unspoken pact with each other from our youth: we would never use drugs. So it made me physically ill to see him not only selling drugs but using them as well, even after he had seen how drugs had devastated everything in our lives.

As for my mother, I was watching her vigilantly to see if her stint in prison had changed her. It didn't take long for me to see that prison hadn't changed a thing. Drinking alcohol was a violation of her parole, but she didn't care. I watched her take drink after drink one evening until she became sloppy drunk and passed out in a chair. The sight disgusted me. I was tired of seeing the people I loved inflict pain on themselves. But there was nothing I could do. When I talked to any of them about changing their lives, they didn't want to hear it. They accused me of preaching and being a "goody two shoes." I learned that you can't help someone who doesn't want to be helped.

One night during my visit, I decided I was going to ride with my little brother and two of his homies. He owned a green 1979 Ford LTD. In the trunk he had two 15" subwoofers and an amplifier that pumped so much bass I'm sure it would measure on a seismograph. The sound system was playing MC Eiht's album, "We Come Strapped." As I sat in the back, the track "Niggaz Make The Hood Go Round" was bumping. We couldn't hear each other over the bass even if we screamed. My brother and his homies were getting high as they passed around a "blunt"—a cigar hollowed out and refilled with marijuana. Suddenly, I had an out-of-body experience.

It felt like I was sitting in a seat outside of the car. I could see the four of us inside. I saw the weed being passed around between my brother and his friends and how high they were. The music put them in a trance. I got scared. I could feel death around us. The music and drugs had taken them to a dark side. I could sense that they were one slight irritation away from being capable of killing. I was freaked out. I'd never experienced anything like that before or since. I knew I had to try to do something to wake Montez up. His life was in danger. I was afraid something bad was going to happen to him if I didn't get through to him.

Over the next several days I tried to talk to him, but the drugs, alcohol and music had control over his mind. He was never sober. Every time I spoke to him I could tell he was getting irritated with me, but I didn't care. He was the only brother I had. I loved him, in some ways, more than I loved myself. But finally, his patience wore thin. He thought I was "dissing" him and making myself out to be better than he. He stood up and shouted in my face, "Fuck you nigga, you ain't nobody!"

Now, I was angry. "You better sit down and get out of my face," I said. He moved closer and stood there breathing hard.

"Man, you better get out of my face," I said again. I pushed him away. He lunged at me and we started fighting. My cousins who were there egged us both on.

My mother yelled, "Frank and Montez, stop it!"

My intention was not to hurt my brother. I was faster and stronger than he was and he knew it. I'd always had the upper hand, and this time was no different. I got him on the ground but he just got angrier. I sat on him for a couple minutes trying to calm him down, but to no avail. Eventually, I let him up and started to run because I knew I only had two options—hurt him or let him wear himself out. He chased me out of the house and up and down the block for 15 minutes. Eventually, his anger subsided. After that, I knew there was no getting through to him. He was going to have to learn the hard way. All I could do was pray for him.

My visit had come to an end and I was heading back to California with a troubled soul. When I left I hugged my mother and brother tighter than I ever had before. I feared that I might never see them again. But there was nothing I could do. My words and love had fallen on deaf ears and hard hearts. I could only show them what a better life looked like through my actions and hope that I could spark the desire in them for something better for themselves.

The Blueprint

In the fall of 1994, I enrolled in two courses and earned two more As. My vision of earning a degree had become more than a fantasy—it was becoming a reality, one class at a time. I just had to be methodical—plan my work and work my plan. I created a strategy where I mapped out the courses I would need to take in order to complete my general education requirements and transfer to a four-year college. I wanted to get a degree in business because I wanted to be just like Uncle Lawrence—the first man I ever loved.

But as I created my plan, I started getting discouraged. If I went to school part-time, it would take me at least ten years to complete my degree. The trouble was, there was no way I could afford to go to school full-time. I was supporting myself financially. But an education was my ticket to redemption. With it, I could finally show the world what I had inside me. But how could I make it happen? One thing was certain: I knew where there was a will there was a way.

That day, in December 1994, I made a vow: I would start saving every penny I could so that I could quit my job at Western Lifts after my five-year anniversary in November 1996 and being going to school full-time starting in the spring of 1997.

Once I committed to my plan and put it into action, the semesters moved swiftly. I stayed focused on my goal and continued to get straight As. I was burning like rocket fuel. As 1996 began, I was on a roll. I was busy every minute of the day. When I wasn't working, I was at school or studying. My blueprint was working beautifully. I was living, breathing, and eating my mission. Nothing else mattered.

But one day in early 1996, I realized that my plan was somewhat flawed. If I waited until the spring semester of 1997 to go to school fulltime, I wouldn't finish my general education requirements until December 1997. Many universities didn't allow junior college students to transfer mid-year. That meant I might not be able to transfer until the fall of 1998. I knew I couldn't afford to sit around until then. I had no choice but to move my quit date from December 1996 to August 1996. That would allow me to transfer to a four-year university, with junior standing, starting in the fall of 1997.

Spring semester started in mid-January of 1996. This was going to be my year. However, I also had to keep saving as much as I could to meet my financial obligations like rent, utilities, my car payment, auto insurance and food. So, I lived like a miser in the months leading up to my quit date.

Everyone at my job knew I was going to school. Most of them didn't understand it and thought I was wasting my time. To them, it didn't make sense that I would take college courses when I already had a good job. I understood that rationale if you believed that working at Western Lifts was the best job you could get. I believed that I hadn't even begun to tap my potential. The only way for me to tap into it was by earning my college degree.

As I got closer to my quit date, I told the two coworkers I trusted most,

Daren and Darrell, about my plans. Not only had they become two of my closest friends at the plant, they were also my two closest friends in San Diego. We had a lot in common. We were all African-American men and all around the same age. Daren was about three years older than me and was married with several children. Darrell—whom we called "Bones"—was about a year older than me, unmarried but with one child.

Daren was from Battle Creek, Michigan and had come to San Diego after joining the Navy. He served four years and didn't reenlist, but like me he fell in love with San Diego and vowed to stay. He was the strongest man I have ever seen. He stood about six-foot-one, weighed 210 pounds, and could bench press more than 400 pounds.

Bones hailed from Birmingham, Alabama. His mother had moved his family from Birmingham when he was in high school, so San Diego had become his home. He was only about five-foot-eight and had a thick southern accent that made him hard to understand at times. But he was a good dude. The three of us would hang out during those rare times when I wasn't at work, at school or studying. We played basketball all the time. It was the bond that strengthened our relationship and because of it, we'd become like brothers.

However, my friends showed different levels of support for my plans. Bones was supportive of me going to school. He had expressed the desire to get an education and create a better financial future for himself and his family. Daren, on the other hand, could be critical. He had his own insecurities and if I actually did something with my life, it would expose his belief that he was unable to do the same.

When I first told Daren I was going to leave Western Lifts to go to school full-time, he responded by saying, "Man, you ain't goin' nowhere." He would repeat this many times during the last six months of my employment, and I would always laugh it off because I knew my time there was coming to an end. But as my quit date approached, I could tell he knew it was really happening. Nothing was going to stand in my way—not even my self-doubts.

Devil's Advocate

About one month before my quit date, I called my mother to let her know what I was doing.

"Hey Mom! How are you?" I said. "I wanted to let you know I'm quitting my job."

"What? What do you mean you're quitting your job? Did you find a better one?"

"No. I'm going to go to school full-time."

I knew my mother. She found the negative in everything and played the role of the devil's advocate better than the devil himself.

"Well, I don't think that's a good idea, Frank. That's a good job and you're lucky to have it."

"You're right Mom. It is a good job. Especially if you can't do anything better. But, I can. I know I can."

"How do you plan to support yourself?"

"Well, I've saved about $8,000 and maybe I'll get student loans," I said with as much confidence as I could muster. I just wanted my mother to support me. I wanted her to hear my dreams and see the vision I had for my life. But it wasn't going to happen on that day.

"Frank, I don't think that's a good idea," she warned. "You have a good job already. You might never make that kind of money again."

She wasn't going to support me on this. Her own insecurities were strangling her; if one of her children actually managed to rise above their failures and make something of himself, it would expose her own faulty paradigm. However, nothing she could say was going to talk me out of my dream. I hung up, discouraged. I was completely alone. I had no support, financial or otherwise. But there was no turning back.

The time had come to execute the scariest part of my plan—to trade in my security for significance—and give Mike my two-weeks' notice. I was deeply grateful for him giving me the job nearly five years earlier, but it was time for me to move on. But before I went to Mike's office, I called Daren and Bones over to my workstation.

"Fellas!" I said. "Today is the day! I'm about to go give Mike my two-weeks' notice."

Bones was smiling. But Daren looked as if he'd just found out someone had died.

"You're really quittin'?" Daren said in a melancholy voice.

"Yeah, man," I replied. "I'm on a mission, brother. I'm never going to be happy unless I do this. This is my destiny."

Bones looked at me smiling. "Handle your business!" he said.

I looked at him in the eyes, "Thank you brother. I will."

Daren just sat there looking at me, still in shock. I excused myself and made my way to Mike's office to deliver the news. After I informed Mike of my decision, I felt a load come off of my shoulders. However, I would be lying if I said I didn't feel some fear, too. I'd been used to the security of a good paying job, and I had just cut away my safety net.

The final two weeks at Western Lifts were bittersweet. Daren was still in shock. Clearly, he felt as if he was losing a brother. We knew we would still see each other because I wasn't leaving their lives. But we were now on separate paths.

My last day finally arrived. As my final 30 minutes ticked away, my co-workers sent me off with a huge water balloon fight. There we were, a bunch of grown men, acting like little boys at work, soaking each other with water. Mike turned a blind eye to it. I think he was sad, too. He was losing his surrogate son and knew he had no choice but to let me go.

At 4:30pm, the horn blew. We cheered, shook hands and hugged. My employment with Western Lifts had officially ended. I was soaking wet as I went to the time clock for the last time. I vowed I would never work any place ever again where a horn told me what to do. I punched my time card a final time and began my final walk through the plant. All of sudden, I heard my name,

"Frank!" Someone screamed.

I turn around to see who was calling me and a water balloon smacked me dead on the side of the head like a rock. It bounced off, hit the floor, and exploded. Everyone burst out laughing. I couldn't help but laugh too. I turned around and continued to walk toward the open dock doors. As I exited, I turned around to look one last time. "Goodbye," I said under my breath. Then I walked out of the building into the light of the summer day.

CHAPTER 16

WALKING IN FAITH

I was attending Mesa College in San Diego. Now as a full-time student and it was exhilarating. On the first day, I jumped out of my bed and prepared myself. I had never felt as much promise as I did on that morning. The sound of the birds singing outside my bedroom window seemed sweeter than ever before. My future was as bright as it had ever looked.

I walked around campus that morning, and there was a buzz of excitement in the air. A new semester brought new goals and hopes with it. While I didn't know exactly what the year would hold, I smiled because I was on a new journey. I had three classes that day and an appointment to visit with an academic advisor. I wanted to be sure my plan to transfer the following fall was tight and that there were no errors that could cause a setback.

As I made the trek from my accounting class to the academic advisement office, I took in the scenery. There were students sitting in the shade at the base of trees, escaping the heat of that warm August day. I noticed something else. From one end of the campus to the other, there was no sign of stress. College life felt like a breath of fresh air to me.

At the academic advisement office, I met my advisor, Brian Katcher. We shook hands. "Follow me," he said. We walked down a long, narrow hallway to his office. We sat down and he wasted no time getting down to business.

"What can I do for you Frank?" he asked.

"Well, this is my first semester as a full-time student and I plan on transferring to a four-year university next fall. I want to make sure I'm on track to transfer with junior standing."

Before I finished my statement, I saw Brian nodding. "Okay. What's your social security number?"

I gave it to him and he typed it into his computer. There was silence as he concentrated on his monitor. Suddenly, he said, "Frank, it looks like you're a business major. Correct?"

"Yes."

"Okay. What school do you plan to transfer to?" he asked, his eyes still locked on the screen.

"San Diego State." I guess my response surprised him because he looked away from the computer for the first time and looked at me.

"Why?" he asked.

Good question. No one had ever asked me that, so I didn't really have a prepared answer.

"Because I live in San Diego," I said, finally.

"Frank, have you ever considered a better school?" he said. "Like Harvard, Yale, Princeton, Stanford, or even USC?"

I laughed out loud. I couldn't help myself. Me in the Ivy League? Hardly.

He was still looking intently at me, so I said, "Everybody in college knows about those schools. They're the crème de la crème. But even if I could get in, how in the world could I pay for it? I'm on my own. I don't have anybody paying for my schooling." I sat silently, confident that would be the end of this discussion.

But Brian looked at me gravely and said, "Frank, you have straight As. With your grades, they'll almost pay you to go. You need to look into some better schools."

Sitting in that office, I had an epiphany. Were my expectations for myself too low? No one ever told me that I could be a real scholar. But here was someone telling me exactly that.

"By the way," he went on, "looking at your academic record, the classes you're enrolled in, and what you plan to take the next two semesters, it looks like you're right on track to transfer as a junior next fall. Let me know if there is anything else I can do for you, Frank."

As I got up from the chair, I thanked him, but my mind was racing. Harvard? Yale? Princeton? Could I actually get into schools like that? Me, a kid from the wrong side of the tracks with a criminal record? Was it even possible?

My head was spinning with the reality that, just maybe, it was.

School Shopping

Over the next several days, my conversation with Mr. Katcher was constantly on my mind. I began to think back to that day in January of 1991 when I first visited Southern California. It had been the first time in my life that I had seen African-Americans (other than the Blankinships) who were successful. They drove Mercedes-Benzes and lived in million-dollar homes. Wealth was commonplace out here and accessible to everyone!

From that first day I laid eyes on Southern California, I knew it was where my dreams were going to come true. Dreaming a little bigger wouldn't cost me anything! So I decided to give some thought to Mr. Katcher's advice. I wanted to stay in California, so Harvard, Yale and Princeton were out. But I was going to look into California schools that were better than San Diego State.

My other challenge was that it was already fall. Admission applications for the following school year were due in less than two months. I began to do research on some of the better-known universities in California. Stanford was the heavyweight, but after doing a thorough review I found out that they didn't have an undergraduate business program. Plus, I wanted sunshine and palm trees along with my success. Northern California was out.

Next came UCLA. I was a huge college basketball fan and the Bruins are college basketball royalty. But UCLA didn't have a true business major, which was what I really wanted. Finally, I turned to USC. I didn't know a lot about the University of Southern California. I grew up in the Midwest and I wasn't a huge college football fan, and USC was known as "Tailback U" for its famous football program. But after researching the university, I began to like what I saw, and they had an undergraduate business program. USC warranted deeper consideration.

To get a better feel for the university and Los Angeles, I enrolled in a half-day program at USC called "Transfer Day", a comprehensive program that gave potential transfer students the opportunity to get additional information on the school and academic life. I sat in on several presentations on the admissions process, transfer credit policies, academics and financial aid. I also took a guided campus tour.

I spent the remainder of the afternoon exploring the campus on my own. On the drive back home to San Diego that evening, I cried all the way home. I'd never seen anything as beautiful as the USC campus and I had never thought I was worthy of such an opportunity. I always felt like I was the underdog kid that nobody ever rooted for and that the good life was out of reach for me. I never thought that an institution with such a storied history and beautiful campus could be an option for me. On that drive, I vowed that no matter how much it cost to go to USC, that was where I would go. Somehow, I believed God was going to make a way.

Trojan

In October of 1996, I completed my application for admission to USC. In March of 1997, with gratitude and pride, I was accepted into the university. However, when I received the financial aid package, I was convinced there was no way I was going to be able to attend. I had applied for dozens of scholarships but nothing had come through. I resigned myself to going to San Diego State.

Then, one day in late spring 1997, I got a letter from USC. With nervous excitement, I tore open the envelope and started reading:

Dear Frank,

Congratulations on your admission to the University of Southern California and the Marshall School of Business. On behalf of our faculty, welcome to the Trojan Family!

I am pleased to inform you that you have been selected to receive a USC Transfer Deans' Scholarship...

That was all I could read before I fell to my knees, clutching the letter in my hands overwhelmed with emotion and shouting, "Thank you Jesus!" That scholarship would make it even more affordable for me to attend USC than San Diego State! I was going to be a USC Trojan. Los Angeles, here I come!

I entered USC in the fall of 1997 as a junior. Unbelievable. I was pinching myself. How I got there I did not know. My only conclusion was that it was all a divine orchestration of God's will. Just six years earlier, I had been fighting for my life in an Iowa courtroom. I felt like I was a lifetime away from that ordeal. My world had changed so much.

However, not everything was wine and roses. Adjusting to the academic rigors of USC was difficult, to say the least. This was the first time that I would be competing in a classroom environment with students who were National Merit Scholars—many of whom were upset that they were "only" attending USC and not Yale or Harvard. They were there because USC had given them a full academic scholarship.

I also felt out of place because of my age. I was 26 years old and going to school alongside kids who were 18, 19 and 20. I was like an old man on campus. Also, many of the kids came from affluent families. While I was always trying to figure out how I was going to make my $230 a month car payment and pay for my insurance, some of these kids were driving around in cars that cost more than four years of USC tuition. Lastly, I was still terribly self-conscious about being a convicted felon. I didn't feel like it was something I could share without being judged. I was ashamed of where I came from and the poverty of my past. I felt like I was pretending to be something I was not. I didn't feel like I truly belonged here.

Most kids, like my first roommate at USC, were getting monthly stipends from their parents. I was working a part-time work-study job on campus from 11pm to 3am, four or five days per week, and living on four to five hours of sleep per day. The workload was monstrous.

By the fourth week of classes in my first semester, I was delirious with fatigue. I was holding on for dear life. One afternoon, on my walk back to my apartment, I called my mother because I just needed someone to talk to. I was trying hard, but 15 credit hours along with work and lack of sleep had taken its toll. She listened to me and—amazingly—was encouraging. She told me, "Keep fighting! It's hard, I know. If it was easy any dummy could do it. You're there for a reason."

I couldn't quit. I wouldn't quit. All my eggs were in this basket. I had nothing else going for me. I had no other options. I was all in. But without a doubt, that first month was the hardest. During the second month, I got a second wind. I began to dig in and get some traction.

I started hanging out with one of the guys in my accounting class, Joe. He was a pretty cool guy with a really good sense of humor. One of the first things he ever said to me was, "Bro, I don't really care for your type, but you're all right." Some people would have been offended by a remark like that, but you just had to know Joe in order to appreciate his sense of humor. Nobody in their right mind would say something like that to someone they don't know unless they were joking.

Joe and I became close friends that semester. We had similar backgrounds. We both grew up rough and believed that somehow we had snuck into USC through the back door. That commonality would be the basis of our friendship. We started hanging out on campus every day. He was somebody with whom I could just be myself. There was no pretending. I came to trust him so much that I shared my secret about being a convicted felon. It didn't faze him in the least. He understood me. As a matter of fact, he one-upped me by sharing that he had served several years in prison. What are the odds? You can't tell me that God doesn't have a sense of humor.

In a land where I didn't feel like I belonged, this friendship helped to take my mind off the glaring differences I had with my other classmates.

Choices

When my first semester at USC came to a close, I finished pretty strong. I didn't receive straight As like I did at the community college, but considering the fact that I had taken USC's best shot, a 3.14 G.P.A. wasn't too bad. I was happy, but not satisfied.

Going into the spring semester of 1998, I was fully acclimated to the culture and competitive nature of the academic system. I knew what to expect, and I knew that I would be able to improve my performance. However, one looming decision that was weighing on me: choosing a business discipline as my major. I was really fretting over it. Make no bones about it; I wanted to make money. The poverty of my youth had marked me, and in my mind money was the most important factor in choosing a major. I hadn't yet learned the lesson that I probably already should have: money should never be the sole reason you do or don't do something. As a matter of fact, I can look back on my life now and say that anytime I have ever made a decision based solely on money, it's almost always been the wrong decision. Unfortunately, poverty has a profound impact on the way you view money. It becomes a totem, a symbol not just of comfort, but of power and significance. The influence money had over my life would prove to be a snare.

I had no real guidance. There was no trusted person in my life to help me make an intelligent decision. Uncle Lawrence would have been a good choice, but he had long since left my life. Joe was in the same predicament. We were both the first college students in our immediate families. Neither one of us had any idea of what to expect from a professional career.

That first semester, we had one accounting class together. Joe got an A- and I got a B+. But I didn't want to do accounting. It didn't seem like a natural fit for me. I had to work too hard just to receive average grades. It just felt as if I was always swimming upstream. I wanted to do something that played to my natural strengths and abilities. I wanted to work in my flow and not against myself.

My gut was telling me to do marketing. I had enjoyed my first marketing class immensely. However, I looked at the salaries for graduates with a marketing degree and I was disappointed. Salaries were in the mid-$20,000 range! There was no way I was going to work as hard as I was and make less money than I had made working at Western Lifts!

Joe was leaning toward accounting and thought I should do the same. "Come on bro," he said. "You should do it, too." I hated the coursework in accounting. But, there was something about the idea of possibly being a CPA that was appealing. "If I could be a CPA," I thought, "people would respect me and wouldn't just look at me as another young black criminal." I still could not get past my felony conviction, and my desperation had me searching for any way to overcome it.

Joe was adamant that accounting was the best undergraduate major in the USC School of Business. Even though I despised the coursework, I saw the benefits. Accounting students didn't have to worry about finding good jobs. Jobs found them. The Big Six (now Big Four) accounting firms like Deloitte and Ernst & Young recruited the top accounting students enthusiastically. To top it off, USC was one of the top five undergraduate accounting programs in the nation at the time. Starting salaries for accounting grads in the big firms were in the mid-to-high $30,000s.

I couldn't find any negatives in doing accounting as a major—except that I hated accounting. But I totally disregarded my feelings in trying to pacify my insecurities. Instead, I explained my apprehension away by telling myself, "I have never been afraid to work hard." Plus, the money would be great. There it was. At the end of the fall 1997 semester, I declared accounting as my major.

CHAPTER 17

CONVICTED FELON

PART 2

When the spring semester of 1998 began, I was a full-fledged accounting student. The infamous beginning coursework for the major was known as "the 350s." The grueling classes that made up the 350s were notorious for causing many a student to reconsider their choice of major and turn to some of the other, easier, majors in the business school. Accounting was not for anyone who wasn't prepared to be challenged, intellectually and physically. But I knew I could make it. The only question was how much pain I would have to endure along the way. There was never a question of quitting. Quitting just wasn't in my DNA.

During the first semester of the program, the Big Six started scouting students as potential hires. Recruiting USC School of Accounting students was a highly competitive process. During this time, the tech bubble of the late 1990s was expanding and the economy was growing at a diabolical (and ultimately, unsustainable) rate. There was a war for talent in the marketplace. The Big Six firms needed to hire plenty of talented interns and graduates as the need for the services the firms offered was booming.

Both public and private firms swarmed college campuses. Universities couldn't pump out accounting graduates fast enough to meet the insatiable demand for talent. Even better for me, forecasts showed that the labor market was going to experience significant shortfalls due to the retirement of the Baby Boom generation. The supply-demand equation was working in my favor. The attitude was up, up and away.

My fellow classmates and I were caught in the middle of this hiring frenzy.

During the semester, I began to get introduced to the "good life". Firms were on campus every day holding information sessions and socials that ranged from pizza parties to private yacht excursions. They were spending millions to impress and influence USC accounting students and get them to choose their company over others.

Recruiting between the firms for interns was competitive. There were a limited number of opportunities and the competition between the students was fierce. Most of the attention went to the best students in the class. Transfer students, to some degree, were at a disadvantage. We hadn't been on campus for several years like the traditional students who'd started as freshmen at USC. They'd had the opportunity to meet with recruiters early on and establish relationships; those same recruiters didn't know who I was.

At the beginning of the spring semester recruiters received a book containing the resumes of every student in the 350s. They were all looking for the same thing: a grade point average of 3.5 or higher. By earning a 3.14 my first semester, I became somewhat invisible to many of the firms.

As a result, I watched the recruiting frenzy mostly from the sidelines. But it stirred up my competitiveness, because I wanted to be courted and wooed too. At the same time, my insecurities reared their head. I was worried that my felony conviction would come up in recruiting. In fact, it was inevitable. I feared that all my hard work and sacrifice would be for nothing because I wouldn't even be able to get past the application process.

Back to Des Moines

I watched all the top students go through the process, excited about the opportunity to receive a prestigious internship with one of the world's leading accounting firms, without having to fear being humiliated. It's a fact that most people fear being humiliated in front of others more than they fear death. I was no different. The Scarlet Letter that I was carrying around with me held me hostage. Secrets keep you sick and the fear of them being revealed only keeps you playing small. I was both sick and small.

Spring internship recruiting finally came to an end, and the semester ended shortly afterward. The lucky few who had been chosen as interns were on their way to an amazing ten-week experience—being wined, dined and catered to. I had one year before I graduated. Something was going to have to give. Or I was going to waste my time, my degree, and my hard work.

However, with my first year at USC complete, I was able to take a deep breath and look around. I reflected on how much I'd learned and accomplished during the past year. My eyes were opened up to things I'd never had any clue about. The knowledge I obtained was transforming my life. I looked at life differently. I had made friends from all over the world. I'd been enlightened. My education was changing me from the inside out.

When summer arrived, I decided I was going to go back to Des Moines. I'd only made brief visits back since October 1991, but this visit was going to be different: I would be staying for three months and living with my mother. Yes, the same woman who had almost cost me my freedom seven years earlier. I wanted to believe everything was going to be okay. But I also knew I had to be on guard. My mother was still dealing crack and if I ever saw any drugs or drug activity, I was out of there. It was a matter of self-preservation.

I arrived in mid-May 1998. It was really good to see my mother. In spite of all that had happened, I still loved her. She had sacrificed so much for my brother and me while we were growing up; she was a fighter who fought until she had nothing left. She was worthy of forgiveness. Even if I had been convicted of the crimes that she perpetrated, I probably would have still forgiven her eventually. Am I a fool? Maybe. But I'm also a son.

My plan was to find a job—two or three, if I could—and work over the entire summer. I didn't have anything else to do. My goal was to save up as much money as I could, return to USC, and finish my senior year.

I started out by going to a temporary agency that provided accounting solutions for companies. This would allow me to put my education to work immediately. But, there I was again, faced with my dreaded felony conviction. Every employment application had the question. There was no getting around it. I decided that I would not disclose it and deal with any consequences that came.

So, when I got to the question on the application, I answered, "No." Without that felony conviction on my resume, I looked stellar. And I knew how to interview. As a matter of fact—up until that point—I had never had an interview where I wasn't offered the job. After completing the employment application, I handed it to the receptionist. She read it and said, "Okay. Let's get you set up on a computer to take the assessment tests." My nerves began to settle after her response. Accounting assessment tests I could handle. I was about to graduate from a top five accounting program. I passed the assessments with flying colors and was ready for an assignment.

My first assignment was at a large health insurance company in the accounts payable department. The company was in the Ruan Center, the second-largest building in Des Moines. I got to dress in business casual attire every day, the office was nice, and there were no roughneck laborers, cursing like sailors, discussing their sexual escapades. "I could get used to this," I thought. Plus, the job was in a climate-controlled environment where I got paid well to sit down. This job was cake compared to all of my previous jobs. I could work double shifts every day and still not be tired. It baffled me to see people talking about how rough their day was. Rough? Accounts payable wasn't even in the same building as rough.

About a week after starting that job, my cousin told me to come down to the YMCA where he worked. They were looking for part-time employees to work with the kids in the evenings during the summer. This really appealed to me. I'd always wanted to be a Big Brother and be able to impact the lives of kids who faced the same disadvantages that I had faced. The best thing I had to offer them—other than my love and compassion—was the experience I had earned through bad choices and mistakes and how I persevered to overcome my setbacks.

I went down to the Y one day after work to meet with the program director. Of course, I was asked to fill out an employment application. By this time, there was no nervousness whatsoever; I knew I was answering "No" to the felony question. No one seemed to check it anyway.

I completed the application and gave it to the program director. Not only did my interview go well, we really hit it off. He ended up hiring me on the spot. I was able to start that same day. This was great news. Now, I would be able to save even more money.

Working with those kids blessed me. I got an opportunity to "pay it forward." Many were underprivileged youths from single parent homes where their parent either worked all day, was on welfare due to addictions or other issues, and couldn't give their children the attention they deserved. I had a lot to offer these kids. I tried to pour as much love and guidance into them as I could in the two to four hours I had with them each day. I would have done it for free if they asked me to.

Scarlet Letter

After six weeks, my assignment at the health insurance company came to an end. I would miss it. The men and women I worked with gave me a card thanking me for all of my help and wished me luck during my senior year at USC.

However, some doors close so better ones can open. By the end of my last day at the insurance company, the temporary agency already had a new assignment for me to start the following Monday at a firm specializing in intellectual property law. I would be doing simple bookkeeping work. The environment wasn't as lively as the health insurance company had been. It was more stiff and sterile. But the job served its purpose and I wasn't going to complain.

My summer was turning out well. I had only a few weeks remaining before I would head back to California to finish my last year of college. Then, one day, I'd finished up at the law firm and headed over to the YMCA. However, as soon as I checked in, Tom, the program director, said he needed to speak with me. I sensed there was a problem immediately, and the sinking feeling in my stomach told me what it was. When I entered his office, I didn't sit down.

"Please shut the door," Tom asked. "Frank," he said seriously. "I got a call today from the administrative offices. They told me they found a criminal conviction that you didn't disclose."

Damn! Am I never going to be free of this?

I looked him in the eyes. "Tom, I'm so sorry," I said. "I'm sorry if I got you in any kind of trouble or made you look bad. I really am."

"I don't have a choice in the matter, Frank," he said. "I'm going to have to let you go."

"I understand. I'm sorry."

I hadn't realized how selfish and self-serving my lying was until then. I think Tom was more hurt to fire me than I was to be fired. But I deserved what I got. He didn't. He deserved better. I promised myself that from that day forward, I would take responsibility for my past and all the consequences. I would be a man of integrity, even if it meant I was going to lose opportunities.

The world was teaching me a lot of hard lessons because in the past, when I felt pressed, all I could think about was surviving by any means necessary. I was learning to allow my actions to dictate my circumstances, and not vice versa. This incident had finally shown me that I could allow myself to always be a prisoner to my lie—waiting for the unfortunate opportunity to be exposed—or I could take control of it. I chose the latter. I also promised myself that if I ever had children, I would always be there. I would always teach them to tell the truth and right from wrong. I would never abandon them.

My summer ended on a sour note. Back at USC, my excitement about completing my last year of college and starting my career had been overshadowed by the fear associated with my felony conviction and how it would affect my prospects for employment. I knew the day where I could hide my felony conviction from prospective employers was over. I also knew now what would happen if I lied about it and got caught: I would be fired. It was time to tell the truth and deal with the consequences.

This turned what should have been a thrilling time into a stressful one. The only time I felt more anxiety was when I was sitting in jail facing up to 60 years in prison. But I was tired of looking back and wallowing in self-pity. I had come to USC for one purpose: to earn my degree. It was time to get it.

Meet the Firms

For a senior, the fall semester in the Leventhal School of Accounting at USC is go time. If you haven't already solidified a job offer with one of the public accounting firms yet, it was time to spruce up your resume and prepare for recruiting. Finding a job in the fall semester is the only thing that matters. If you don't, the only jobs remaining will be Plan B opportunities, and nobody wants to settle for Plan B.

Recruiting started right from the beginning of the semester. The Big Six accounting firms had become the Big Five due to a merger and they were on campus early and often. That semester, I was navigating 17 units of coursework, five firms, and severe anxiety.

One of the first big social events for students and prospective employers was the Meet the Firms event. In the ballroom at the USC Town and Gown building a huge hors d' oeuvres table occupied the center of the room, with display booths for companies around the entire perimeter. Dozens of recruiters and the firm's employees were present to meet with students who were focused on doing one thing, finding a job. The ballroom was packed like sardines and the non-stop chatter was deafening. Everywhere you looked there were men wearing suits, white shirts and nice ties. The women wore black skirts, white shirts and close-toed shoes. That was the uniform.

I hated attending these functions. It was like a cattle call with the firms looking for the best steer. To say I felt out of place was an understatement. I didn't come from a family that wore suits and ties. If you had a collar in my family, it was blue. Heck, I didn't even own a suit until I got to USC. I felt like I was walking on eggshells. I was afraid I was going to shake someone's hand the wrong way or say something inappropriate. But I knew I had to do this.

The real problem I had wasn't with meeting the firms. The problem was my fear in letting the firms meet me. However, that's what they were going to have to do. I had to go forward with the process and deal with the fallout from my past. Living in my head was killing me.

However, having a naturally gregarious personality, it didn't take me long to warm up. Before I knew it, I was working the room like a master. Communicating with people was my forte—starting a conversation with a complete stranger had always been easy for me. So it turned out that I was in my element. Before the night was over, I had opened up the door to a potential full-time employment opportunity with the head recruiter for Arthur Andersen, Jenny Buchbinder. Arthur Andersen had an impeccable reputation as a firm. That would change after the Enron scandal, but at the time, if you worked for them, you could pretty much write your own ticket.

After spending a significant amount of time speaking with Jenny, I was motivated to go and meet other firms. As the event concluded, I felt pretty good. I felt like I made some solid connections that I could work over the next few events in the hopes of landing a job.

When I was leaving the ballroom that evening, I ran into Ms. Buchbinder from Arthur Anderson again. Before I knew it, I was spilling my guts to her—telling her about my felony conviction! I never had the courage to share my secret with a potential employer before. It's not like I had some game plan about how to approach it; I just dropped a bomb on her. It felt like asking a girl to marry me on the first date. She listened intently and then responded.

"Thank you for being honest and forthright, Frank," she said. "I appreciate that. I'd really like to interview you. However, I'm going to have to speak with my boss about whether or not your situation will prohibit it. I have your resume. I will call you in a couple of days once I find out. Is that fair?" I nodded and then stood dumbfounded. Either she was a good actor or she really cared about trying to see beneath the surface.

I thanked her for her time and the care and concern she showed me, and we parted ways. I felt like there might be hope for me after all. I was proud of myself for being truthful. In fact, the evening was exhilarating for me in a lot of ways. I was starting to feel like God hadn't made a mistake in guiding me here, like I was supposed to be here all along.

Several days after the event, I walked into my apartment after class and one of my roommates gave me a message that a woman from Arthur Andersen had called. Her number was written on a piece of paper by the telephone. I immediately dropped my bag and went over to grab the note. As I held that little piece of paper in my hand, I was extremely nervous. I swallowed hard and took the note into my bedroom and closed the door to call her back.

I sat on my bed next to the phone for several minutes. Fear pounced on me and smothered my thoughts. What if she says no? I was terrified to pick up the phone. This wouldn't just be about Arthur Andersen; it would be a preview of how most any reputable company would react to the revelation about my past. Everything hinged on this call.

But of course, I couldn't sit there forever. I picked up the phone and began to dial her number. As the line rang, I panicked. I wanted to hang up but I couldn't. I didn't want her to think I was playing games. The line rang a second time; I was having a hard time breathing. In the middle of the third ring, she picked up.

"Arthur Andersen. Jenny speaking."

I froze. "Hello?" she said again.

I stammered, "Uh. Hello. Ms. Buchbinder?"

"Yes. This is Jenny," she said in a cheerful tone.

"Um…hi, Ms. Buchbinder. This is Frank Thomas. I received a message that you called. How are you today?" I was, just barely, keeping my voice from trembling.

"I'm okay, Frank. How are you?"

The cheerful demeanor in her voice suddenly lowered. I began to sense this wasn't going to be a great call.

"I'm doing okay, too," wishing that I could be anywhere in the world but on the phone. Heck, prison didn't sound so bad. It would be less humiliating. "I wanted to return your call," I said.

"Thank you for doing it so quickly. I spoke with my boss about your situation. Unfortunately, Frank, there's nothing we can do," she said. I could feel the sorrow in her response. There was an awkward silence.

What does this mean for me? My body and mind went numb.

"I understand," I said. "Ms. Buchbinder, thank you for taking the time to hear me out and to see what you could do. That means a lot to me."

"Frank, the pleasure was all mine. I wish it could have been better news. I wish you the best of luck," she said warmly. I thanked her one last time and said goodbye. I could hear the receiver on her end hang up as the line went dead. Dead. That's exactly how I felt. Who was I trying to fool anyway? My life was a joke.

Darth Vader

After that call I fell into a depression. It was my senior year of college. I was supposed to have the world by the tail. Instead, all I could think about was my future—my lack of one. I had spent so much time, energy and money. I'd shed so many tears over the years and made so many sacrifices to position myself to achieve my dream of getting a college degree. Now, it looked like the stupidest decision I could have made. No one was going to give a convicted felon an opportunity to work for one of the most prestigious firms in the world.

Part of me wanted to check out. I had to force myself to remember that I had never quit at anything. I reminded myself that I've never controlled the outcome, only the input. Within a short time, I'd snapped out of my funk. I was not going to live in pity. That's not who I was. I'd come this far, and I was going to see this thing through to the end. My college degree was my prize. No one could deny me that.

My attitude shifted back to the positive and upbeat person I had always been. Even in the darkest periods of my life, I had believed that God was going to see me through. Miracles had already occurred in my life. I wasn't going to let a small setback end my journey. I re-engaged with college life and I once again I was all-in.

Recruiting season went on. Yes, one firm had denied me, but there were others. I pressed on. I went to every recruiting event to meet the decision makers of those remaining firms. At every event, I would see Jenny Buchbinder and my courage would drop a notch. She would always smile at me but no words were ever really exchanged. Actually, she made me nervous. She knew my secret. I feared she would tell all the other recruiters about me. Worse, I feared that I would become the center of rumors and gossip. But I never had any indication that she had said a word to anyone.

I continued campaigning for full-time positions, but now I played my cards close to the vest. I wasn't going to reveal anything until I absolutely had to.

Then I met Charlie Osaki, recruiter for Deloitte & Touche. Charlie was the number one recruiter among all the firms. He had an air of confidence that no other recruiter possessed, and his status was legendary at USC.

Around the USC campus and many of the other university campuses throughout the region, Charlie was known as "Darth Vader". When it came to interviews, he was reputed to be the toughest of the tough. If Charlie chose to interview you, you knew you were the cream of the crop. Deloitte almost always got their man or woman if Charlie wanted them. He was that persuasive.

I was terrified of speaking with Charlie. I didn't think a guy like that would ever understand my circumstances. His confidence bordered on arrogance and gave him the bearing of an elitist. I wasn't in the same zip code as the elite; I was a poor kid from a family of drug addicts, drug dealers, and alcoholics, and I feared that my past would confirm all his presumptions about me. I had no business dealing with someone like Charlie Osaki.

Oddly enough though, Joe (my best friend at USC) had come to know Charlie and hit it off with him pretty well. Charlie really liked Joe. I hoped that this blossoming friendship would lead to an introduction to Charlie. But I didn't dare ask Joe to introduce me because I knew he had his own criminal record to overcome, and I'm sure he was stressing about that. I didn't want to put my buddy in a situation where he might feel uncomfortable or jeopardize his opportunity to land a job with Deloitte. If a firm was going to hire a convicted felon, I couldn't help but believe that one was the maximum. They weren't in the business of criminal rehabilitation.

I did end up with an introduction to Charlie Osaki, but it came from one of the only other African-American students in the accounting program, Rodney Davis. Rodney had interned with Deloitte in the firm's tax department the past summer, and I had shared a little bit of my past with him. He trusted me. During a football tailgater hosted by Deloitte, he connected Charlie and me. The rest was up to me.

After some initial small talk, I could tell Charlie knew at least something about my past. Rodney, obviously, had given Charlie a heads up. While I was nervous about that, I was also relieved. I thought, "If Charlie already knows the ugliest part of my story and is still willing to speak with me, that has to be a good sign." So, I decided to just tell him everything.

I started at the beginning and never stopped. Charlie never interrupted or asked questions. He simply listened and shook his head at several points. When I finished speaking he said, "I don't know how a kid goes through what you've gone through, leaves the Midwest to move to Southern California on his own and finds his way to USC. But, it's not by chance. You're a winner."

Charlie was impressed at the fight that I had within me to overcome my past. From that day on, Charlie was an advocate for me. He advised me to go through the entire recruiting process with every firm and told me that I could expect to interview with Deloitte. But he couldn't promise me anything. Still, a door was open and I was thankful.

My first interview with Deloitte, I presumed, would be with Charlie. It was not. It was with another representative of the firm's recruiting team. Charlie had the power to "green light" me past the on-campus interview, but he didn't. He refused to show me one ounce of pity or preferential treatment, and I appreciated that. I wanted to earn my way because I deserved it, not because someone liked my story or felt sorry for me.

Based on the result of my on-campus interview, I was invited to interview with Deloitte in-house. Over the course of the fall semester, I got interviews with the three remaining Big Five firms: KPMG, Ernst & Young, and PricewaterhouseCoopers. When all was said and done, I had four offers of employment. However the other three did not know about my felony conviction. Deloitte & Touche was the only firm who extended an offer of employment to me despite my criminal record. I remain grateful for that to this day.

It was a victory—God's victory. In late October of 1998, I accepted an offer to join Deloitte & Touche's Assurance and Advisory Services practice in the Los Angeles office. Deloitte had accepted me based on what I had accomplished, not based on my worst mistake. They believed in second chances.

I felt overwhelmed with joy and appreciation. I may not have had the world on a string, but I was definitely sitting on a rainbow. I was thankful that God had created a path and an opportunity for me—another miracle. I had learned a vital lesson: just because you fail doesn't mean life is over. No matter what your failure is, you must rise and fight on!

God had known my heart when I sat in that county jail in a fight for my life. When I confessed His son, Jesus Christ, as my personal Lord and Savior, I promised Him that if He gave me another chance, He would never have to worry about me again. Ever since that low point of my life, He has been making a way for me. And I'll never stop praising Him.

CHAPTER 18

REDEEMED

Now that I had landed a job and my next few years seemed to have a firm foundation, I had to focus on the task at hand—finish my academic courses. I couldn't get lackadaisical just because I had employment. Deloitte could rescind their offer to me if my final grades didn't meet their standards. So, I worked to make sure that didn't happen.

Each spring semester, the staff and faculty of the Leventhal School of Accounting at USC host a competition to select one student from each program—bachelor's and master's in accounting and master's in business taxation—to represent their graduating class as the student speaker during the commencement ceremony. Candidates have to be nominated by their classmates. Nominees who are interested in competing have to prepare a seven-to-ten-minute speech to be delivered one evening before the start of the final examination period. A panel of judges then chooses one person to represent their class and deliver the student commencement address at the graduation ceremony.

I didn't think anything of the competition because I had no desire to speak in front of a huge audience. So I was stunned when the staff and faculty approached me to see if I would be interested in competing and informed me that I had received the most nominations from my classmates. My fear said no, but my heart said yes. My heart won.

During the last two weeks of the semester, I worked on a speech. I tried to compose something that I felt would best represent my class and describe our journey. The emotion of the process caught me by surprise. I poured my soul into each word. But I knew I still had to deliver a great performance if it were to be heard.

The evening of the competition, I delivered my speech with all the feeling I had. After the judges deliberated, I was informed that I had won the competition; I would represent the graduates of the Bachelor of Science program at graduation! I couldn't believe it. I was going to give my family, fellow classmates and their families, and the staff and faculty of the Leventhal School of Accounting a speech my soul had been longing to share my entire life. My experience at USC was coming to a close more wonderfully than I could have ever dreamed.

Finally, graduation day arrived. I couldn't help but reflect on my past and how far I'd come. The pain had been almost unbearable; the work, emotionally exhausting. I'd fought for 27 years to stand here as somebody who deserved to win because I was willing to fight to the end.

How had it all happened? How had I defied the odds? I paused and looked to the sky with tears in my eyes and said, "Thank you Lord. Thank you for never giving up on me. Thank you for never letting me lose hope." This was one of the greatest days of a life that had seen more losses and darkness than victories. I was finally free.

The Speech

I was only the second person in my family to ever graduate from college and the first in my generation. Several of my family members had flown in to attend and everyone was bubbling with excitement. In many ways, this was a defining moment for all of us. The pain our family carried—from the effects of racism, discrimination, alcoholism, drug addiction, poverty, violence and fear—was powerless on this day. We all stood together on one accord, in unity, with love. On this day, our family had hope and a future.

But there was one person missing: my Uncle Lawrence. His absence disappointed me. He was the closest thing to a father I'd ever had and I thought he would be the proudest of all. In fact, all I had ever wanted to do was make him proud of me. But we hadn't spoken in almost ten years. Once I left Kansas City, I felt like he pretty much gave up on me. Once I'd been arrested for selling drugs, he wouldn't touch me with a ten-foot pole. To this day, our relationship has never recovered. But, I still have a great amount of respect for him. If it weren't for him, I wouldn't have ever had the vision to rise above my circumstances. Not only did he give me a positive male role model, he also introduced me to God. For both, Uncle Lawrence, I'll never be able to repay you.

However, even my disappointment couldn't darken the day—Friday, May 14, 1999. The weather was sunny and beautiful. The campus was bustling with graduates dressed in caps and gowns, accompanied by proud family and friends. My family members and I smiled with delight as I took them on tour of the campus. Along the way, I would stop to share the significance of one of the buildings or to take a picture with one of my classmates. It was absolutely magnificent.

Before long, the members of my undergraduate class began to line up outside of Bovard Auditorium to begin the ceremony. As our commencement speaker, I had the honor of leading the processional into the auditorium—a very proud occasion for me. We walked into the auditorium to "Pomp and Circumstance" and took our seats. It was surreal. None of it—the graduation, the fact that I was the speaker, my hiring by Deloitte & Touche—had sunk in yet.

Kenneth Merchant, the dean of the Leventhal School of Accounting, walked to the podium to speak about the achievements of the class. It was captivating. As I listened, waiting to deliver my speech, thoughts about what this day represented began flooding my mind. Silently, I asked God, "Why am I here? There are so many other people who deserve to accomplish this who will never get the opportunity. Why do I?"

I'd traveled so far. I'd overcome so much fear and doubt. I had to find incredible mental, physical and spiritual fortitude just to arrive at this day. How did I make it? My thoughts were interrupted when I heard my name being called. The time had arrived for me to make a statement for myself, my family, my fellow classmates and the staff and faculty.

I rose and walked to the podium. I could see my family sitting in the first several rows. This is what I said:

Today is a great day for us all, because it signals the beginning of a group of promising futures. However, most importantly, it is a signal of no more homework, no more midterms and final exams, and no more $20,000 tuition checks. We've reached a great destination in life's journey. But, it has not come without personal sacrifice and perseverance.

I can remember when we, students, started the program; the infamous 350's. The 350's were the beginning of the Accounting declaration and the end of our colleges social lives. I had heard of the term "all-nighter" before, but the 350's defined it. I do not think any of us had ever worked so hard in our lives.

Through sharing a common struggle, we became family. We spent hours in the basement of Leavey Library in collaborative workrooms, stuffed like sardines taking turns working problems preparing for our midterms. Then, someone would run to the coffee shop on campus and bring back pounds and pounds of junk food. And we would work into the daylight hours riding a sugar high. Stopping on several occasions to laugh because it seemed as though the more the night wore on, the sillier we got.

And then, there were the notorious group projects. These were great learning experiences in themselves. There was always somebody in your group that never pulled their weight. And you guys know who you are.

But for the most part, we learned to work together. Being such a distinct group, we learned to bridge the gap between our religious, racial, gender and cultural differences that make us unique and appreciate our diversity.

Yes, we worked hard, but we played hard, too. Our classroom ties manifested outside the classroom. Once we were classmates. And now, we are friends. Through membership in several of the accounting organizations on campus, we enjoyed several firm-sponsored and organization-sponsored events. Through these events, we have made contacts in the accounting field and our bonds have grown even stronger.

But, today, we have come to a crossroad in our journey. Our hard work and diligence has helped us to achieve the greatest goal to date in our lives. It's not how hard you push along the way. It's about having something in you to finish. And finish we did.

Today, we should all be proud of our achievements. But we cannot rest on yesterday's accomplishments. The achievement of our greatest goals spurs the evolution of new goals. What was our future four years ago is now upon us.

Now, we are faced with decisions regarding our immediate futures. The opportunities available to us are vast. Although many of us already *know what is next for us, in the future lies uncertainty. Where are we headed? What are we going to do be doing in one year? Five years? These questions enter our minds. However, do not fret, for these questions enter the minds of everyone in this room—from the youngest of our siblings all the way up to faculty that taught us what we know. For we have been armed with a solid foundation that will help us to succeed in whatever we may choose.*

Success. Success is a word common to us all, yet it has so many different meanings. Success is not about how big your house is, the kind of car you drive, or the amount of wealth you accumulate. Success is a state of mind. If you possess a positive state of mind in achieving your goals, all of those other things will fall right in to place.

I am proud of myself. I am proud of you. I am proud of us for all that we have achieved. I am proud because we did not scare when faced with what seemed to be unachievable tasks—because I can remember so many of the causalities that we had along the way. We did not let the idea of a little hard work and sacrifice scare us away from achieving our goals. And this is a characteristic we will carry into every endeavor from here. Never be afraid to work hard. Never let a few obstacles get in the way of accomplishing your goals.

I want to say thank you to our parents for supporting us—for listening to our complaints and giving us encouragement. To our professors, who challenged us to think outside the box and forced us to push our limits. And last, but not least, the accounting school staff for keeping the screws from coming loose. Together, we make the Leventhal School of Accounting. It is through the work of us all that this day is possible.

In closing, I know many of us sitting here have mixed emotions. We are happy that we are graduating today, completing our four-year mission of higher education. But, there is a part of us that is sad that our lives will take separate paths. Sad that we will never share these experiences as a group again. Be happy for the blessings we've shared together because we have a place in time—a place that no one can ever take away from us. I will hold thoughts of our struggles, triumphs, and laughter close to my heart forever and I pray that you do too.

I love you, Mom.

When the ceremony concluded, I led the recessional from Bovard Auditorium to the courtyard in the front of the building. Friends, family and faculty stood saluting us for a job well done. As I waited for my family, many people—some I knew and many I did not—approached and thanked me for giving such a heartfelt and powerful speech. I was overwhelmed. When I spotted my family exiting the auditorium doors, I hugged every one of them. But I saved my mother for last. As we embraced, the tears flowed. The joy was overpowering. Nobody but us knew all that we had to overcome to stand in that moment. Nobody knew the struggles we'd endured.

After many tears and a long hug, we collected ourselves. My mother looked at me in the eyes and said, "Son, I'm proud of you."

With all the confidence and strength I could muster, I responded, "Mom. If you're proud of me now, you ain't seen nothing yet!" In that moment, I realized that your past does not define your destiny unless you allow it to and people are greater than their circumstances. We can always rise above them.

ACKNOWLEDGMENTS

No one does anything significant alone. I've been blessed by many people who have given and sacrificed for me so that I might complete this work.

To My Lord and Savior, Jesus Christ: Thank you! You captured my heart when it was hurt and hard. You gave me new life. Now, I rise in You.

To my beautiful wife, Erika: God blessed me beyond measure when He gave you to me. Thank you for your love, patience, encouragement and sacrifice, and for allowing me the space to heal, grow, and do the work I've been called to do. Next to Jesus, you're my rock! I love you always and forever!

To my wonderful children, Sydney and Kellen: Your births changed me. When I look into your eyes, I know I can't live small. I want God's best for your lives, and I know the only way for you to receive it is for me to be a role model by being obedient and pursuing God's best in my own life. Walk in faith always! Never be afraid to stand in the truth of who you are in Christ Jesus! I love you! Joshua 1:9

Charles Osaki: Thank you for seeing the winner in me. You stuck your neck out when there was nothing for you to gain and everything to lose. I'll never forget that.

Deloitte & Touche: Thank you for giving me the opportunity to change my story in a world where it's difficult to get a second chance. Your reputation for hiring only the best has opened doors for me that would have otherwise been shut. I'll always be a proud alum and promise to represent the firm to the best of my ability.

Cheryl and Chuck Childress: Mom and Pops, thank you for taking me in and loving me as your own, even when I wasn't lovable. You saved my life. I'll forever be indebted to you. I love you both dearly!

David Childress: You're my brother for life. I love you, man!

Michael McNearney: I know you've passed on but I never got the opportunity to thank you. You never knew my story. You only knew me, the man. Thank you for trusting my work ethic and giving me the opportunity to lead beyond my years. I'll never forget you. Rest in peace, my friend.

Uncle Lawrence: You gave me a vision of authentic manhood. But more than that, you introduced me to God. Because of that introduction, when darkness came and I had nowhere else to turn, I called on Him and it changed everything. Thank you for standing in the gap for me when I needed a father figure most. I love you.

Tim Vandehey: Remember when I asked you if you believe in divine appointments? You're one for me. This book was never going to be finished until you arrived. Thank you for tearing it up and helping me rebuild it stronger and more powerfully. I can hardly wait to get started on the next one. Thank you!

Robert Dwyer: Thank you bro! You're a foxhole friend and down until the end. I love you man.

Carlos Veliz: You have the biggest heart of any man I've ever known. I thank God for bringing you into my life. I love you man.

To my brother, Montez: We've been through a lot together. You're not only my brother; you were my first best friend. I love you.

To my dad: What can I say? You're my dad and without you I have no story. I love you no matter what. God bless you.

To the family, friends and colleagues who impacted my life but I didn't recognize by name: You have taught me so much about life. I thank God that He has blessed me by your lives. My only prayer is that in some small way I made a fraction of the impact on you that you have made on me. God bless you and keep you always.

A special thank you to the 142 people who so believed in the power of my story that they contributed to my Kickstarter crowdfunding campaign to ensure this book was published.

And an extra special thank you to the Kickstarter contributors below who went above and beyond in a major way. Your financial generosity and ability to see my vision are the reasons this book exists:

KICKSTARTER

Donors

Gold Level - $250+

Brooke White and David Ray

Reed Stanley

Jennifer Hankes Painter

Karina and Pete Deckard

Chrislynn and Glenn Freed

Aida and Jose Peralta

Frene and Ian Chestnut

Paul James

Irma and Richard Gancze

William Chang

Sandy and Charles Osaki

Yoon Jin and Jason DeVilliers

Ruben Nava

Dennis Thomas

Monica & Robert Trautwein

Platinum Level - $500+

Marie Rosales

Steve Kizito

Nita and Lamar Booker Jr.

Diamond Level - $1,000+

Robert Dwyer

Dana and Joseph Jundt

Melinda & Pedro Biezonsky

G.L. Blankinship III

Carlos Veliz

Double Diamond - $5,000+

Mark Plimpton

Finally, to my mom: The past is gone. I know you did the best you could. That's what matters to me. You're a warrior in my eyes. I got my strength from you. No matter how many times you've been knocked down, you still rise! You're my hero. I love you.

RISE

OFFICIAL MERCHANDISE

RISE T-SHIRTS - $24.95 PLUS S&H

The RISE T-Shirt is a high quality American Apparel poly-cotton short sleeve crew neck. Poly-Cotton (50% Polyester / 50% Combed-Cotton) construction. The perfect 50/50 blend that creates a soft and comfortable slim-fitting T-shirt. Unlike other t-shirts, American Apparel is made with combed cotton, giving it an ultra soft, worn in feel and a superior drape. Sizes S to XXL.

Front: "RISE Even Death Can't Stop Me – Proverbs 24:16"
Back: "When life has you down the only thing to do is RISE"

RISE WRISTBANDS - $3.99 PLUS S&H

RISE EVEN DEATH CAN'T STOP ME
WWW.THEFRANKTHOMASSTORY.COM

The RISE wristband is a 100% silicone dual layer color engraved wristbands with a 1/2" width. These bands are made with two colors, black on the outside of the wristband and white on the inside of the band and within the lettering. The dual layer color and engraving make them even more eye-catchy.

ORDER NOW AT WWW.COACHFT.COM

QUANTITY DISCOUNTS AVAILABLE

Frank Thomas

coach consultant speaker

A coach, consultant and speaker who cares about your personal, professional and business success

coaching consulting speaking

COACHING

Let's face it; making changes that lead to greater success in your life, career, or business can be daunting and scary. Managing change requires an experienced guide who can support you through the process. When it comes to business, career, and life coaching, Frank Thomas understands your challenges and leads you to success.

Frank offers a wide range of individual and group coaching plans designed to help clients reach their potential. If you're serious about reaching your peak contact Frank for your complimentary coaching session and get on the path to greater success.

CONSULTING

Business consultants like Frank Thomas possess the experience and skills that enable companies and their employees to do what they do best, successfully run their business. Frank's experience and professional background working with some of the world's largest companies gives him a depth and breadth of knowledge surpassed by few.

Frank consults companies in a wide range of areas that position them for greater success. Contact Frank today if you have a vision for your company but need an experienced consultant to partner with you to make it a reality.

SPEAKING

Frank Thomas has captivated and inspired audiences at Fortune 100 companies as large as The Walt Disney Company to institutions of higher learning, non-profit organizations, and faith-based organizations on topics ranging from diversity and inclusion and other human resource management challenges to leadership, overcoming obstacles and other areas of personal development.

Frank delivers messages that are powerful, pragmatic, and transformational. If you need an inspirational speaker with a commanding presence but a common touch to drive home your vision, values, or mission, contact Frank Thomas about speaking at your next event.

CONTACT

For more information about Frank Thomas or to sign up for his free trainings, seminars and other resources please visit www.coachft.com.